STRUCTURAL MODELS IN FOLKLORE AND TRANSFORMATIONAL ESSAYS

APPROACHES TO SEMIOTICS

edited by

THOMAS A. SEBEOK

assisted by

DONNA JEAN UMIKER

10

1971

MOUTON

THE HAGUE · PARIS

STRUCTURAL MODELS IN FOLKLORE AND TRANSFORMATIONAL ESSAYS

by

ELLI KÖNGÄS MARANDA

and

PIERRE MARANDA

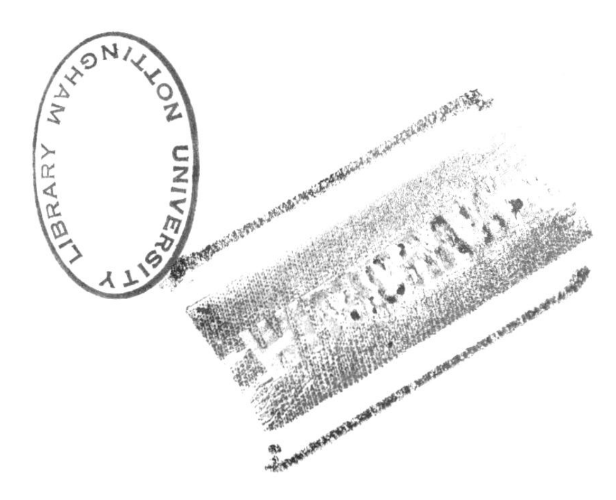

1971

MOUTON

THE HAGUE · PARIS

LIBRARY OF CONGRESS CATALOG CARD NUMBER: 79-141183

Printed in The Netherlands by Mouton & Co., Printers, The Hague.

to Erik and Nicolas

TABLE OF CONTENTS

I. TOWARDS THE INVESTIGATION OF NARRATIVE COMBINATORICS: INTRODUCTION, by ELLI KÖNGÄS MARANDA 11

II. STRUCTURAL MODELS IN FOLKLORE, by PIERRE MARANDA and ELLI KÖNGÄS MARANDA 16
0.0 Definition of structure 16
0.1 Definition of folklore. 16
0.2 Distinction between a folkloristic item and its record . . 17
0.3 Principal approaches to folklore 17
0.4 Structural studies of folklore 18
0.5 Units suggested previously 21
0.6 Parameters 22
1.0 Our hypothesis 23
1.1 The theory 24
1.2 Our interpretation of Lévi-Strauss' formula 30
1.2.1 Application of the formula. 30
1.2.2.0 Units. 31
1.2.2.1 Terms 32
1.2.2.2 Functions. 34
1.2.2.3 The interplay of terms and functions . . . 34
1.2.2.4 Summary of our analytic units. 34
1.3 Our cause-effect formula 35
1.4 Our models. 35
1.5 Materials used 37
2.0 Zero mediator (model I) 37
2.1 Lyric (sonnet). 38
2.2 Lyric (song of repetition) 42
2.3 Lyric (song of repetition) 46
2.4 Preliminary conclusion 48
3.0 Failing mediator (model II) 49

3.1 Sage 49
3.2 Interconnectedness of different aspects of one item. . . 52
4.0 Successful mediation : nullification of the initial impact (model III) 52
4.1 Sage 53
4.2 Sage 55
4.3 Magic 57
4.3.0 Charm as a part of the healing act 57
4.3.1 Sebeok's analysis 57
4.3.2 A complementary analysis 59
4.3.3 Implications for the analysis of rituals. 63
4.4 The three first models 65
5.0 Successful mediation : nullification of the initial impact as a means of increasing on the initial state (model IV) 66
5.1 *Schwank* 66
5.2 *Schwank* 68
5.3 *Schwänke* and riddles 70
5.4 Myth 71
5.5 Sage 73
5.6 Sage 76
5.7 Riddle 78
6.0 Proverbs 80
7.0 Superstitions 81
8.0 Experimentation. 83
9.0 Conclusions. 86
9.1 Use of recordings 86
9.2 + and — 86
9.3 Mirror picture structures 87
9.4 Initial binary oppositions 87
9.5 Mediation 87
9.6 Differences in the outcome 88
9.7 Morphology of models 88
9.8 Lyric, narrative, and ritual 93
9.9 Taxonomic limitations 93
9.10 Structure and psychosocial function 93
9.11 The use of Lévi-Strauss' formula 94

III. Of Bears and Spouses : Transformational Analysis of a Myth, by Pierre Maranda 95
1. Operational concepts 95

1.1 Equivalence 96
1.2 Analogy 96
2. Of bears and spouses 98
2.1 M_1, Netsersuitsuarssuk 98
2.2 M_2, Sigfitusuarssuk, who killed a bear with his stick 102
2.3 Comparison of M_1 and M_2. 104
2.4 A transformation to pass from M_1 to M_2 and vice versa 107
2.5 Residues. 108
3. Test of the approach 109
3.1 M_3, The woman who heard bears speak 109
3.2 Second transformation rule to pass from M_1 and M_2 to M_3 112
4. Summary and conclusion 114

IV. "A Tree Grows": Transformations of a Riddle Metaphor, by Elli Köngäs Maranda 116
1. Materials 116
2. Riddle metaphors 116
3. Simple riddle 119
4. Transformations 121
4.1 Transformations, Series I: Expansion 121
4.2 Transformations, Series II: Reversal 126
4.3 Transformations, Series III, IV: Complementary sets, Inversion 130
5. Conclusion 135

Bibliography 140

I. TOWARDS THE INVESTIGATION OF NARRATIVE COMBINATORICS: INTRODUCTION

ELLI KÖNGÄS MARANDA

The essay reprinted here was intended as a sketch which we at the time of writing, in 1962, wanted to develop further. A number of the ideas have been in the meantime elaborated by one or the other of the authors, working on other materials, other genres, other tradition areas. We have also spent two years in Melanesia, in a predominantly pagan society where myth and ritual are fully alive and form the core of the culture. The wealth of the new materials collected — roughly estimated, 12,000 pages of texts, over a thousand riddles, several hundred magic formulas, and perhaps 200 hours of storytelling and music on tape — is so great and the task of preparing them for publication, translating, annotating, correlating, analyzing, is so urgent that it seems impossible for us at present to return to the materials of this essay. We have therefore decided to correct only the printing mistakes which marred the first edition, and to make but a few slight alterations and additions to the text as such. On the whole, the exposition is left untouched. It is fitting to do so also in order to allow the original ideas, however germinal and underdeveloped, to speak for themselves. We restrained ourselves even from inserting Lau examples, first, because of the great distance between them and the examples here used; secondly, because most of Lau narratives are so long that they could not be quoted in this space without serious distortion; thirdly, because considerable background materials would be necessary for any interpretation.

Some general observations can, however, be reported. We lived in a society where knowledge is money and those who know in fact cash in. Performing a sacrifice, a cure, or protective magic, or singing the sacred epics (*'ai-ni-mae*, literally 'the root-of-the death') of a clan can bring rewards which compare favorably with what a man working 'overseas' on a coconut plantation would save in a year. The epics are well known by many, but they cannot be performed by just anybody.

Rather, the specialists have a knowledgeable audience, well aware of the operations performed. Here is a first point which we wish to stress : that to live and maintain its richness, oral literature, like other arts, rests on the audience, on its reactions, its criticism and its encouragement, and that without a knowing and sophisticated audience any lore soon turns moribund. This is of course what von Sydow spoke of when he discussed active and passive carriers of tradition. In modern terms, one would here see folklore as communication, narratives (and other items) as messages, storytelling as information transmission, storytellers as encoders, audience as decoders, the language of myth as intertwined codes, and differences between generations as noise. (Köngäs Maranda, 1963b, pp. 84-126).

Yet we are not, on the basis of our recent experience, totally convinced that all recitals are intended for information transmission. In Lau society, there is much information exhibiting, and often so performed that the decoder is prevented from learning the item. Thus, for example, the names of ancestral villages have their poetic variants, as such lyrics of several lines. A full recital of an *'ai-ni-mae* will contain the poem in case of each occurrence of a place name. But our epic singers would guard their knowledge by reciting those poetic parts so fast that they became unintelligible. For our collecting purposes, those poems were separately and privately given — classified information if you wish. This even that the place names are so abundant that the danger of an unauthorized snatching by the audience would be in our opinion unlikely : one epic-singer, for example, was able to list and relate to other locations 1,551 place names. He knows them because he masters the *'ai-ni-mae*, and, of course, he masters the *'ai-ni-mae* for one reason because he knows the onomastic lore.

This man had in his youth made an intentional 'grand tour' of the sacred places in order to learn the geography and history of his world. He had done so acting on the advice of his mother's brother who had been to Queensland in the labor trade and upon his return described white men and their power, and who had become convinced that a 'white peril' threatened also Malaita. Ramoagalo, our man, concluded that the threat was based on white man's knowledge, and set to expanding his own. By his inherited social position and by his personal intelligence and vast knowledge he is perhaps the most prominent Lau man; we also saw him ward off a hurricane by appropriate magic. Local trust in him and in the tradition were once more strengthened when his village stood untouched next to a devastated Christian village.

If this was our historian and theologian, Bobongi, one of the nine chiefs of Marching Rule, was our verbal artist. Like other leaders of the nativistic movement, he was sentenced to prison for six years. We collected several dozens of lengthy narratives from him; many of these he had learned from another 'agitator' during the peak of Marching Rule, when the leaders moved about in Malaita on their mission, dangerous in the view of the colonial government.

But how can a man learn an hour-long story "from Wane Dili during the Marching Rule, when we slept in the bush"? Mainly because he only expands his knowledge of combinatorial possibilities. He has long before learned his basic stock of building elements, such as genealogies, classes of supernaturals and their 'realms of action', etc. He also has a store of problems suitable for use as initial situations, topics such as the origin of mankind (as seen from his universe), the origin of diversity of languages (in native theory, adopted by the British administration, there are about a dozen languages in Malaita), the origin of social organization, the origin of each clan — a problem activated in the great feasts when the history of the celebrating clan is sung — the origin of taro, of yam, of coconut, of pig, ceremonially regulated foods; origins of diverse clan-specific ('totemic') food taboos and other important regulations of social life. Such problems are answered by the epics, but the combinatorics is not static, even plots are not identical, and the problems are not answered always in the same manner. The singers of the epics, and the tellers of secular tales, make their decisions: this decision-making is in outline as described in our tree diagram below (Ch. II. 1.4), only it involves a lot more detail. The singer's choice of terms, functions, mediators, and outcomes either satisfies the audience — when their ancestors are glorified or at least not sold short — or, as we at times witnessed, causes 'scandals' when there are persons present whose glory is stolen.

The history and prehistory of the celebrating clans is not the only transformer of Lau plots. Another one, to take a concrete example, is the context in community life in which an epic is presented. Even the codes vary: when recited for its informative value, the *'ai-ni-mae* can be told; when recited in a ceremony, they are sung, thus employing two codes, music and a specialized language. We had a unique experience of hearing one epic on consequent days presented twice by one performer, a woman. In the first occasion, she 'told' the story. The recital lasted almost exactly one hour, was replete with place and ancestral names and other 'hard facts', all geared to give (or exhibit) information. While she was finishing her session, in fact answering questions of interpretation, a messenger rushed to the scene to bring the news of a young woman's death. The storyteller, a competent mourner, left for the wake. At the wake, she sang the next day the same story to the vocal accompaniment of the other women gathered to mourn. The recital was after two hours interrupted by the arrival of some near relatives and the hysteric wailing that ensued. She had now omitted almost all factual information and had now systematically exploited all possible tragic aspects of the narrative. The difference between the two performances was discussed afterwards with another member of her community, a man, who pronounced both renderings good "because when she tells the story she has to tell what she knows, and when she sings at a wake, she has to make people cry".

Among the passive carriers we had persons passive as to sacred lore although well versed in it, and active as to 'neutral' *(mola)* lore. These would be the critics: people who at least theoretically mastered the rules of composition and some of whom were quite articulate and outspoken. Yet we must stress the distinction between folkloric and linguistic messages; although in both domains actual utterances take place on performance level and in both domains the audience and even the performer criticizes (as well as builds) the performance according to a competence model, the competence models of narratives (and other folklore items) are much harder to map, because the units are much bulkier than in language. Any linguist can any day gather a corpus of non-sentences, utterances which are pronounced wrong and corrected on the spot by the speaker himself or for example by the parent of a language-learning child; but how many folklorists or anthropologists have ever collected a narrative which was criticized and corrected or in any way signalled out as a 'non-myth'?

Despite the differences due to the size of both maximal and minimal units, linguistic and folkloristic messages have many traits in common. A language-learner, such as a small child or a foreign speaker, resorts to 'ready-made' units, sentences and phrases learned by heart while striving to master the rules of sentence-building. Further, there are stock phrases, such as greetings and many others, which even competent speakers use without recreating them. But for most of the things one makes the utterances from pre-existing units following the combinatorics of his language. We are presently inclined to see narratives and even more stylized genres, such as riddles, as less stable messages than usually thought. Myths and other narratives, and for that matter other genres, are perhaps never learned 'by heart', but the stability which can be discovered is due to the strictness of the combinatorial rules used.

We have supplemented the original article with two more recent essays, one by each author. The new articles may perhaps at first glance seem unrelated, but are each to be considered attempts at mapping transformations, one in a corpus of narratives, the other in a corpus of riddles. And a transformational analysis, to us, is a natural step from the investigation of the structures of folklore 'at rest' to studying them 'in motion', in the dynamic processes which are the essence of folkloric communication.

We wish to express our thanks to those who contributed comments and suggestions either in the germinal phase of the essay or after the publication of the first edition. Among the former are the members of Thomas A. Sebeok's seminar on structural analysis in folklore in 1962 at Indiana University. Among the latter we wish to mention especially Claude Lévi-Strauss, Jerome S. Bruner, Dell Hymes, Suichi Nagata, Philippe Richard, and Bernard Jaulin. Only we are responsible for the statements we make, however.

II. STRUCTURAL MODELS IN FOLKLORE

PIERRE MARANDA AND ELLI KÖNGÄS MARANDA

0.0 DEFINITION OF STRUCTURE

Structure can be defined as the internal relationship through which constituent elements of a whole are organized. Structural analysis thus consists of the discovery of significant elements and their order.

0.1 DEFINITION OF FOLKLORE

Since analogous structures can possibly be found in other classes of phenomena than folklore, folkloristic structures are conditioned only by the limits of the concept of folklore. In this paper, we have used a tentative definition which can, in a compact fashion, be stated thus: FOLKLORE IS UNRECORDED MENTIFACTS.[1] One of the corollaries is that no text as such is a real folkloristic item: texts are only records of mentifacts (whereas an artifact always is its own record). This has practical bearing on the investigation of texts, because the structure of a folkloristic item may not become manifest in the recorded text, but its use, *e.g.*, the magician's action, may be part of the item.

[1] Elli-Kaija Köngäs Maranda, "The Concept of Folklore", *Midwest Folklore* XIII (1963), 69-88. A discussion of the concept of folklore is not possible in this connection; we wish only to point out that this definition considers the field more delimited than it is defined in Sigurd Erixon's *folklivsforskning*, see *Folkliv*, I (Stockholm, 1937), pp. 5-12, but, on the other hand, broader than it is defined in many statements about 'oral literature', *e.g.*, Melville J. Herskovits, "Folklore", in Maria Leach (ed.), *Dictionary of Folklore, Mythology, and Legend*, I (New York, 1949), 400; Francis Lee Utley, "Folk Literature: An Operational Definition", *Journal of American Folklore* LXXIV (1961), 193-206.

0.2 DISTINCTION BETWEEN A FOLKLORISTIC ITEM AND ITS RECORD

It follows then that there are different kinds of fragmentary pieces: those which the informant did not master completely, and those in which the recording was insufficient. One has, of course, to content oneself with the information which is available; but one should bear in mind that no recording is complete, not even a video-tape recording, since the actual situation in which folklore is presented is the only environment in which it can live. That means that the tradition-carrier and his audience, their actions and reactions, the language used and its connotations, the whole of the group's culture should be known before any accurate analysis of a given folkloristic item is made possible. That such requirements are impossible to meet does not effect their validity; and scholarship would certainly gain reliability if the limits of its possibilities were acknowledged.

0.3 PRINCIPAL APPROACHES TO FOLKLORE

Our presupposition is thus, also, that many points of departure and many methods resulting from them are useful in the study of folklore; in fact, not only useful, but also necessary. Some such basic points of departure would be structure, content (themes), style, and function. All of these are aspects of the same item, which naturally means that they are interconnected. In the course of this study, we have, for example, found that there is in our models a definite slot for the 'message' of the item in question, *i.e.*, the psychosocial function. This slot is to be found in the last member of our two last formulas; we will point it out in connection with these models. It is, indeed, of interest to discover that a model which is an abstract representation of one aspect contains nonetheless a point of articulation to the whole social phenomenon.[2]

[2] "Nous avons représenté les systèmes de classification comme des 'arbres'; et la croissance d'un arbre illustre bien la transformation qui vient d'être évoquée. Dans ses parties inférieures, un arbre est, si l'on peut dire, puissamment motivé : il faut qu'il ait un tronc, et que celui-ci tende à la verticale. Les basses branches comportent déjà plus d'arbitraire : leur nombre, bien qu'on puisse le prévoir restreint n'est pas fixé d'avance, non plus que l'orientation de chacune et son angle de divergence par rapport au tronc; mais ces aspects demeurent tout de même liés par des relations réciproques, puisque les grosses branches, compte tenu de leur propre poids et des autres branches chargées de feuillage qu'elles supportent, doivent équilibrer les forces

0.4 STRUCTURAL STUDIES OF FOLKLORE

In some fields closely connected with folklore, such as social anthropology and linguistics, structural analysis has been used with success. In folkloristics, the approach has gathered momentum in the present decade. After the earlier pioneering works of Vladimir Propp,[3] Claude Lévi-Strauss,[4] and Thomas A. Sebeok,[5] a relatively large array of articles

---

qu'elles appliquent sur un commun point d'appui. Mais, au fur et à mesure que l'attention se déplace vers des étages plus élevés, la part de la motivation s'affaiblit, et celle de l'arbitraire augmente : il n'est plus au pouvoir des branches terminales de compromettre la stabilité de l'arbre, ni de changer sa forme caractéristique. Leur multiplicité et leur insignifiance les ont affranchies des contraintes initiales, et leur distribution générale peut s'expliquer indifféremment par une série de répétitions, à échelle de plus en plus réduite, d'un plan qui est aussi inscrit dans les gènes de leurs cellules, ou comme le résultat de fluctuations statistiques. Intelligible au départ, la structure atteint, en se ramifiant, une sorte d'inertie ou d'indifférence logique. Sans contredire à sa nature première, elle peut désormais subir l'effet d'incidents multiples et variés, qui surviennent trop tard pour empêcher un observateur attentif de l'identifier et de la classer dans un genre'' (Lévi-Strauss, *La pensée sauvage* (Paris, 1962), pp. 210-211).

As to the interplay of STRUCTURE and CONTENT in our analyses, it might also be clarified by drawing an analogy with what Chomsky concludes, on linguistic analysis, about the interplay of form and content : "These counter-examples should not, however, blind us to the fact that there are striking correspondences between the structures and elements that are discovered in formal, grammatical analysis and specific semantic functions .... It seems clear, then, that undeniable, though only imperfect correspondences hold between formal and semantic features in language. The fact that the correspondences are so inexact suggests that meaning will be relatively useless as a basis for grammatical description ....

"The fact that correspondences between formal and semantic features exist, however, cannot be ignored. These correspondences should be studied in some more general theory of language that will include a theory of linguistic form and a theory of the use of language as subparts .... Having determined the syntactic structure of the language, we can study the way in which this syntactic structure is put to use in the actual functioning of language .... We can judge formal theories in terms of their ability to explain and clarify a variety of facts about the way in which sentences are used and understood. In other words, we should like the syntactic framework of the language that is isolated and exhibited by the grammar to be able to support semantic description, and we shall naturally rate more highly a theory of formal structure that leads to grammars that meet this requirement more fully." Noam Chomsky, *Syntactic Structures* ('s-Gravenhage, 1962. [Second Printing]), pp. 101-102). And see below, 3.2.

[3] Vladimir Propp, *Morphology of the Folktale* (Publication Ten of the Indiana University Research Center in Anthropology, Folklore, and Linguistics), ed. Svatava Pirkova-Jakobson, transl. Laurence Scott (Bloomington, 1958).

[4] Claude Lévi-Strauss, "The Structural Study of Myth", *Journal of American Folklore* LXVIII (1955), 428-444, reprinted in Thomas A. Sebeok (ed.), *Myth: A Symposium* (Bloomington, 1958), 50-66 and rewritten in French by the author,

on different folkloristic genres has now appeared.[6] Lévi-Strauss himself has almost completed and for the best part published his monumental

with some modifications, as Ch. XI of *Anthropologie structurale* (Paris, 1958); "La Geste d'Asdiwal", Extrait de *l'Annuaire 1958-59* (Paris, École Pratique des Hautes Etudes, Section des Sciences Religieuses, 1959), 3-43; *Leçon inaugurale* faite le mardi 5 janvier 1960, *Collège de France*, chaire d'anthropologie sociale (Paris, 1960), partly reprinted under the title "Problèmes de l'invariance en anthropologie", *Diogène* XXXI (1960), 23-33; "La structure et la forme", *Cahiers de l'Institut de science économique appliquée* XCIX (1960) Série M. No. 7, 3-36, also under the title of "L'analyse morphologique des contes populaires russes", in *International Journal of Slavic Poetics and Linguistics* (1960), 122-149; "Four Winnebago Myths: A Structural Sketch" in Stanley Diamond (ed.), *Culture in History* (New York, 1960), 351-362; *La pensée sauvage* (Paris, 1962). — Among the very first papers inspired by Lévi-Strauss' method stand out: Marcelle Bouteiller, "Cosmologie et médecine magique selon notre folklore rural: Esquisse d'analyse structurale", *L'Ethnographie*, N.S. LIII (1958-59), 91-95; Edmund R. Leach, "Lévi-Strauss in the Garden of Eden: An Examination of Some Recent Developments in the Analysis of Myth", *Transactions of the New-York Academy of Sciences*, Series II, Vol. XXIII (1961), 386-396. *Cf.* Rodney Needham, *Structure and Sentiment* (Chicago, 1962).

5 Thomas A. Sebeok, "Cheremis Dream Portents", *Southwestern Journal of Anthropology* VI (1950), 273-285; "The Structure and Content of Cheremis Charms", *Anthropos* XLVIII (1953), 369-388; Thomas A. Sebeok and Louis H. Orzack, "The Structure and Content of Cheremis Charms", Part II, *Anthropos* XLVIII (1953), 760-772; Thomas A. Sebeok and Frances J. Ingemann, "Structural and Content Analysis in Folklore Research", in *Studies in Cheremis: The Supernatural (Viking Fund Publications in Anthropology* XXII*)* (New York, 1956), 261-268; Thomas A. Sebeok, "Sound and Meaning in a Cheremis Folksong Text", in *For Roman Jakobson*, Comp. Morris Halle, Horace G. Lunt, Hugh McLean, and Cornelis Van Schooneveld (The Hague, 1956), 430-439; Thomas A. Sebeok, "Folksong Viewed as Code and Message", *Anthropos* LIV (1959), 141-153; "Decoding a Text: Levels and Aspects in a Cheremis Sonnet", in Thomas A. Sebeok (ed.), *Style in Language* (New York, 1960), 221-235.

6 Matti Kuusi, "Omaistenvertailukertaus", *Kalevalaseuran vuosikirja* XXXVIII (Helsinki, 1958), 89-108; *Idem*, "Kansanparadokseista", *Kalevalaseuran vuosikirja* XLII (Helsinki, 1962), 56-68. Alan Dundes, "Brown County Superstitions", *Midwest Folklore* XI (1961), 25-56; *Idem*, "From Etic to Emic Units in the Structural Study of Folktales", *Journal of American Folklore* LXXV (1962), 95-105; *Idem*, "The Binary Structure of 'Unsuccessful Repetition' in Lithuanian Folktales", *Western Folklore* XXI (1962), 165-174; *Idem*, "The Morphology of North American Indian Folktales", *FF Communications* 195 (Helsinki, 1964). Robert A. Georges and Alan Dundes, "Toward a Structural Definition of the Riddle", *Journal of American Folklore* LXXVI (1963), 111-118. Daniel Ben Amos, "The Situation Structure of the Non-Humorous English Ballad", *Midwest Folklore* XIII (1963), 163-176. John L. Fischer, "The Sociopsychological Analysis of Folktales", *Current Anthropology* 4 (1963), 235-295. Claude Bremond, "Le message narratif", *Communications* 4 (1964), 4-32; *Idem*, "La logique des possibles narratifs", *Communications* 8 (1966), 60-76. Charles T. Scott, "Persian and Arabic Riddles: Language-Centered Approach to Genre Definition", Supplement, *International Journal of American Linguistics* 31 (1965).

Mythologiques,[7] Leach has written some articles and edited a symposium.[8] And secondary, critical literature on Lévi-Strauss and Propp has started.[9]

In the meantime, transformational analysis has gained ground in linguistics and is spreading its influence to folkloristics;[10] such distinctions as that between deep structures and surface structures contain a promise for the analysis and understanding of oral literature.

Violette Morin, "L'histoire drôle", *Communications* 8 (1966), 102-119. Also the papers in Pierre Maranda and Elli Köngäs Maranda (eds.), *Structural Analysis of Oral Tradition* (Philadelphia, University of Pennsylvania Press, 1970): Claude Lévi-Strauss, "The Deduction of the Crane"; Edmund R. Leach, "*Kimil*: A Category of Andamanese Thought"; Dell Hymes, "The 'Wife' who 'Goes Out' like a Man: Reinterpretation of a Clackamas Chinook Myth"; A. Julien Greimas, "The Interpretation of Myth: Theory and Practice"; Victor Turner, "The Syntax of Symbolism in a Ndembu Ritual"; James L. Peacock, "Class, Clown, and Cosmology in Javanese Drama: An Analysis of Symbolic and Social Action"; Alan Dundes, "The Making and Breaking of Friendship as a Structural Frame in African Folktales"; Elli Köngäs Maranda, "The Logic of Riddles"; Roberto da Matta, "Myth and Anti-Myth Among the Timbira"; and Pierre Maranda, Alan Dundes, Edmond R. Leach and David Maybury-Lewis, "An Experiment: Notes and Queries from the Desk, With a Reply by the Ethnographer".

7 Vol. I, *Le cru et le cuit* (Paris, Plon, 1964), Vol. 2, *Du miel aux cendres* (Paris, Plon, 1967), Vol. 3, *L'origine des manières de tables* (Paris, Plon, 1968).

8 Edmund R. Leach, "Lévi-Strauss in the Garden of Eden: An Examination of some Recent Developments in the Analysis of Myth", *Transactions of the New York Academy of Sciences*, Series II, XXIII (1961), 386-396; *Idem*, "Genesis as Myth", *Discovery* (May 1962), 30-35; *Idem*, "The Legitimacy of Solomon: Some Structural Aspects of Old Testament History", *European Journal of Sociology* 7 (1966), 58-101; *Idem* (ed.), *The Structural Study of Myth and Totemism (A.S.A. Monographs)*, (Edinburgh, Tavistock, 1967).

9 On Propp, see Bremond's paper in footnote 6 and his "La postérité américaine de Propp", *Communications* 11 (1968), 148-164; A. Julien Greimas, *Sémantique structurale* (Paris, Larousse, 1966) Ch. 4; see also Dundes' works in footnote 6 for applications. On Lévi-Strauss, see Leach's papers in footnote 8; Philippe Richard, "Analyse des *Mythologiques* de Claude Lévi-Strauss", *L'Homme et la Société* (juillet 1967), 109-133 and (avril 1969), 179-191; the papers in Leach (ed.), *The Structural Study of Myth and Totemism*; Dan Sperber, "Le structuralisme en anthropologie", in Oswald Ducrot *et al.* (eds.), *Qu'est-ce que le Structuralisme*? (Paris, Seuil, 1968); also special issues of or papers in the following journals, *Esprit*; *L'Arc*; *Annales*: *Économies, Sociétés, Civilisations*, and Buchler and Selby, *A Formal Study of Myth* (Austin, 1969).

10 Elli Köngäs Maranda, "The Logic of Riddles", in Pierre Maranda and Elli Köngäs Maranda (eds.), *Structural Analysis of Oral Tradition*; Elli Köngäs Maranda, "Structure des énigmes", *L'Homme* 9 (1969), 5-48; *Idem*, "Perinteen transformaatiosääntöjen tutkimisesta" [Transformation rules in oral tradition], *Virittäjä* 2 (1970), 277-292. Also I.R. Buchler and H.A. Selby, *A Formal Study of Myth*, Vinittäjä (1970), p. 138ff, which, however, does not discuss transformations of entire items but of personages. Before these, Propp proposed series of the transformations in "Les transformations des contes fantastiques", in T. Todorov (ed.,) *Théorie de la littérature* (Paris, 1965), 234-262.

0.5 UNITS SUGGESTED PREVIOUSLY

One of the primary problems of any structural study is to find operational units, *i.e.*, elements which can be manipulated and on which logical operations can be done (such as reductions, products, summations, transformations, etc.)[11]

Units, or elementary constituents, are the parts which can be isolated in a continuum, for example a narrative, and which cannot be analyzed into smaller forms within the adopted system of investigation.

Examples of units suggested in previous folklore studies are:

type (Aarne, 1910),
function (Propp, 1928),
motif (Thompson, 1932),
mytheme (Lévi-Strauss, 1955),
motifeme (Dundes, 1962).[12]

TYPES, as Propp already remarked, are defined by the presence of striking moments and not on the basis of their 'construction'; such moments may or may not be structurally significant. MOTIF, similar to type, only a smaller unit, as such has no operational value (for a decisive criticism of motif as a unit, see Propp; Saporta and Sebeok, and cf. below, 0.6).

MYTHEME is a contentual-structural unit (see Lévi-Strauss, "La structure et la forme") which consists of the relationship between a subject and a predicate in which the analyst rewrites a myth's components; it is exemplified abundantly throughout Lévi-Strauss' *Mythologiques*.
FUNCTION and MOTIFEME refer to the same concept, "an act of dramatis personae which is defined from the point of view of its significance for the course of action of a tale as a whole".[13]

Other ways of devising units of analysis have been suggested, such as focusing on the pauses made by the storyteller (Pool; Powlinson), and such as defining (1) temporal span and significant contingencies (Saporta and Sebeok), or (2) units of behavior (Armstrong), or (3)

11 Pierre Maranda, "Anthropological Analytics: Lévi-Strauss' Concept of Social Structure", in Hugo Nutini and Ira R. Buchler (eds.), *The Anthropology of Claude Lévi-Strauss* (New York, Appleton, Crofts, 1971).
12 A discussion of these and other units can be found in Dundes, *Morphology of North American Indian Folktales*, Ch. III.
13 Propp, *Morphology of the Folktale*, p. 20; see alse Dundes, "From Etic to Emic Units", pp. 101 and 103.

analytic propositions (Powlinson; Maranda; Labov and Waletzky).[14] Each of us has recently done extensive work with such fine units, Maranda with analytic propositions in computer analyses of myths, Köngäs Maranda with the storytellers' pause-marked units in field collecting of Melanesian myths. Although fine units are valuable also for the overall analysis of a narrative, they have in fact little to do with structure as we use the term in this monograph. Here, we deal with gross analytic units. But automatic analysis can group fine units to reveal exactly those gross units; this would correspond to Lévi-Strauss' way of determining bundles of relations and their interconnectedness and, from another angle, to Bremond's Propp-inspired narrative models.

0.6 PARAMETERS

Motifs, floating intercultural narrative elements, are comparable to phonetypes in linguistics. For a structural study of plots, the 'phonemes' of the corpus have to be found. This can be done, as in language, only by studying the organization of the corpus itself and by defining the differences which make a difference, those features that are distinctive. One can describe sounds of a language out of context, but without it one does not know if the description is relevant. It is for such reasons that international, intercultural, interlanguage, intercorpus 'motifemes' are fallacious. However, generally valid methods for discovering the units of each corpus can be developed and, perhaps, general parameters on which the distinctions rest can be revealed. Methods of this type would correspond to Jakobsonian distinctive feature analysis. We are of the opinion that Lévi-Strauss has pointed out some such parameters, *e.g.*, hunter/hunted, container/contained, left/right, up/down, etc. And Maranda, in the construction of dictionaries for automatic analyses, resorts to 'verbs' or functions like transitive/intransitive motion,

[14] I. de Sola Pool in *Idem* (ed.), *Trends in Content Analysis* (Urbana, Ill., 1959), 202-206; J.L. Powlinson, "A Paragraph Analysis of a Yagua Folktale", *International Journal of American Linguistics* 31 (1965), 109-118; S. Saporta and T.A. Sebeok, "Linguistics and Content Analysis", in Pool (ed.), *Trends in Content Analysis*; P. Maranda, "Computers in the Bush : Tools for the Automatic Analysis of Myths", in J. Helm (ed.), *Essays on the Verbal and Visual Arts* (Seattle, 1967); *Idem*, "Formal Analysis and Intra-Cultural Studies", *Social Science Information* 6 (1967); W. Labov and J. Waletsky, "Oral Versions of Personal Experience", in Helm (ed.), *Essays on the Verbal and Visual Arts.*

intrinsic/extrinsic transformation, etc. We must remark that the number of such parameters is not yet known, nor has it been defined when they pertain to terms and when to functions (cf. Bremond's attempts in this direction).

For European folktales, during the work which is briefly summarized below (Sect. 8), Köngäs Maranda established a basis for distinctive feature analysis of terms. In märchen, only the age, sex, and social status of the terms is given; for all the rest, the actors are defined solely by their actions. Thus a personage in a European folktale is always defineable by a triad, as represented by the corner points of the following diagram.

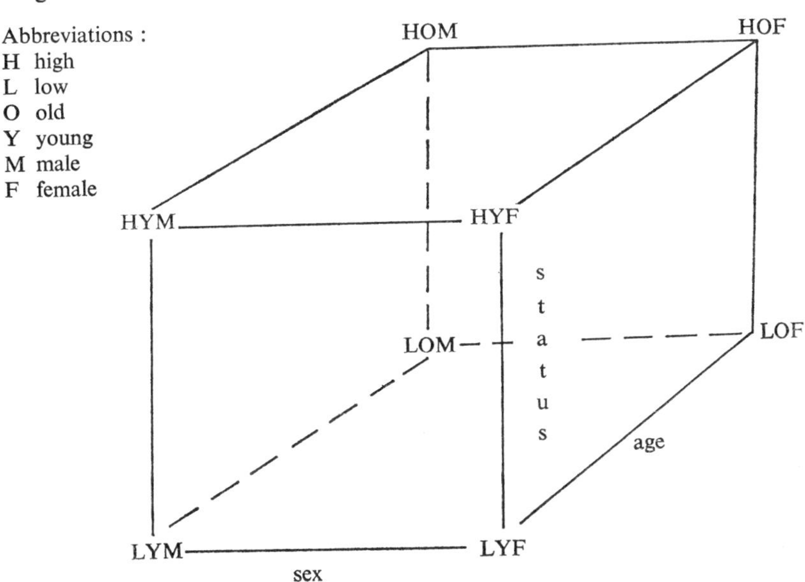

1.0 OUR HYPOTHESIS[15]

Our working hypothesis has been to check a restricted application of Lévi-Strauss' formula[16] and, as implied in his approach, the binary processes of folkloric thought, against cases of different folkloric genres.

[15] This paper is a result of a thoroughgoing cooperation in that its working hypothesis was first elaborated through different tentatives conducted by the authors and then coordinated in detailed discussions which at times were tape-recorded; we tried also, in each case, to develop our applications independently in order to test results against each others' findings. Finally, the article was written together.

[16] As in *Anthropologie structurale*, p. 252. N.b. In Lévi-Strauss' article in Thomas A. Sebeok (e.d.), *Myth: A Symposium*, there is a typographic ambiguity, p. 64.

1.1 THE THEORY

According to Lévi-Strauss, the mythical mind[17] establishes a web of relationships between socio-historically given facts and it works on a symbolic level underlaid by the interplay of infra- and super-structures.[18] It thus performs the specific task of mediating irreducible opposites. This conforms to the pattern of conciliation of opposites, *coincidentia oppositorum*, through a mediator, which other students of symbolism consider as the constant dynamic core of mental processes.[19] A structural

[17] On the controversial interpretation of the "mythical mind" by Leach, see J. Pouillon, "L'analyse des mythes", *L'Homme* VI (1966).

[18] *Anthropologie structurale*, 364 ff; *La pensée sauvage*, Ch. IX.

[19] In the course of an anthropological analysis of binary kinship structures along lines developed by Lévi-Strauss, here is what R. Needham states on this subject: "The empirical starting point is that the expression of symbolic opposition in dualistic classifications is found extremely commonly in human culture. The most general and frequently observed manifestation of dualistic ordering is the distinction and differential evaluation of right and left, best exposed in Hertz's classic paper, in which he maintains that dualism is of the essence of 'primitive thought' ..., and illustrated in a vast array of evidence compiled by Wile .... Hocart treats of this and related oppositions under the rubric of life and death, also concerning himself with the fundamental nature of dualistic order and its world-wide extent ...; and Rassers exploits the same kind of dualistic order, characterized incidentally by the opposition of right and left, in his studies of Javanese myth and drama .... Of a similar nature is the opposition between sacred and profane, so emphasized by Durkheim, van Gennep, and Hertz; and as a final example I would cite the work of Dumézil in the analysis of the Indo-European conception of sovereignty in terms of complementary opposites .... Dualism is manifested in symbolic classifications throughout the world, and all periods of history, with such constancy (though with varying degrees of elaboration) as to lead one to ascribe to it a natural and perhaps logically necessary character.
The important common feature of these dualistic representations is not simply duality but the relation of opposition between the terms (notions, values, classes, etc.) The prime importance of this notion has been underlined by its long philosophical history in the west, from Pythagoras and Heraclitus onwards. Aristotle regarded opposition as one of the categories of human thought (*Categories*, chs. X, XI), and the opposition of truth-values has for centuries received recognition in traditional logic as one of the 'laws of thought', the law of the excluded middle. In a philosophical work which Durkheim and Hertz both cite in their researches into forms of classification, Hamelin maintains indeed that opposition is the fundamental logical feature without which no thought would be possible: ' "En dehors du fait primitif de l'opposition des contraires et, par suite, de leur conciliation synthétique, il n'y a pas de procédé pour constituer la pensée' .... To the same effect, I should claim that in order to think at all we must distinguish, and that the simplest form of distinction is opposition. It is this simple logical fact, I think, which is the ground for the universality of dualistic schemes of classification..." '

"In the particular classification we are examining, however, it is not simply antithetical opposition which is the rationale (cf. Zoroastrianism), but a particular mode of opposition, viz. COMPLEMENTARY opposition. Lastly, it is clear that this cannot in itself constitute a system of representations; and in order to relate pairs of opposite terms into a system we require a further principle, that of ANALOGY. This type of analysis should then be centered upon first discovering in the item itself pairs of opposites and a mediator capable of including them.[20] Mediation can be roughly reduced to a metaphoric structure[21], but this would not meet the criteria of descriptive adequacy as we shall see presently. In effect, analogy — of which metaphors are a case — is essentially 'linear'. Continuous analogy, A : B : : B : C, "A is to B as B is to C", or discontinuous analogy, A : B : :C : D, "A is to B

relation may also be claimed as indispensable to thought (Dorolle, 1949), and as such is a further ground for the universal character of dualistic classification." Rodney Needham, "A Structural Analysis of Aimol Society", *Bijdragen tot de Taal-, Land- en Volkenkunde* CXVI (1960), 103-104.

Gestalt psychology has had a strong impact on structuralism (see for instance, C. Lévi-Strauss, *Les structures élémentaires de la parenté* [Paris 1949], p. XIV; *Anthropologie structurale*, p. 354). Here is the viewpoint of a genuine Gestaltist, along lines not alien to those sketched by Needham :

"Bipolar organization occurs not only when we observe what others are doing. Rather, anybody may find himself directed toward, or away from, particular objects in a way which involves the same kind of dynamic pair-formation. In fact, apart from states of lowest vitality, there is hardly a total field from which bipolar organization is absent. The self is virtually always directed toward something or away from it. The most striking instances are those of intense emotions and motivations .... Obviously, bipolar organization resembles situations in physics in which lines of force or directed processes refer one part of a field to another. In Gestalt Psychology the various directed attitudes of the self are not interpreted as 'instincts' which reside in the self *per se*. Rather they are regarded as VECTORS, which depend both upon the self and upon given objects, or more precisely, upon the relation which obtains at the time between the characteristics of the former and those of the latter. This is, of course, entirely in line with the way in which physical vectors between objects depend upon the 'characteristics-in-relations' of these objects. The various states of the self which are here involved are to a high degree determined by physiological conditions within the organism....

"The play of psychological vectors, the sources from which they spring, the stresses which some parts of the field suffer under their influence, the various changes which are so caused, and eventually the cessation of vectors and stresses when certain results have been obtained — all this is the major study of psychology, as it is the major content of life" (W. Köhler, *Gestalt Psychology* [New York, 1959], pp. 176-177).

From the standpoint of developmental psychology, which modifies the Gestaltist approach, see Jean Piaget, *La formation du symbole chez l'enfant* (Paris, 1945); *Idem, La psychologie de l'intelligence* (Paris, 1947); *Idem, Les relations entre l'intelligence et l'affectivité dans le développement mental de l'enfant* (Paris, 1958).

See also Lévi-Strauss, *Anthropologie structurale*, pp. 133-183; Ad. E. Jensen, *Mythos und Kult bei Naturvölkern* (Stuttgart, 1951); Mircea Eliade *Traité d'histoire des religions* (Paris, 1953); Clyde Kluckhohn, "The Scientific Study of Values" in *3 Lectures* (Toronto, 1958); P. Radin, H. Frankfort, etc., etc. ...

[20] These 'impossible' situations would be expressed by such pairs as, *e.g.*, life versus death, birth from the ground versus from a human couple, earth versus water, parents versus children, etc., C. Kluckhohn, "The Scientific Study of Values", pp. 43-49.

[21] On metaphorical and metonymical poles, see Roman Jakobson and Morris Halle, *Fundamentals of Language* ('s-Gravenhage, 1956), *passim*; Claude Lévi-Strauss, *La Pensée sauvage*, pp. 70, 140-141, 198-199, 271-277, 280-283, 297-302, 319.

as C is to D", cannot formalize the twists found in myths and which call for a 'non-linear' formalization (see below, this section, the quotation from *L'origine des manières de table,* but see also the use to which analogy is put in the transformational analyses by Maranda and by Köngäs Maranda in this volume).

Lévi-Strauss' formula,

$$f_x(a) : f_y(b) :: f_x(b) : f_{a^{-1}}(y)$$

should be understood as the figuration of a mediating process where some dynamic roles are expressed more accurately than in a simple analogy model. In this formula, (b) is the mediator; (a) is the first term, which expresses, in connection with the socio-historical context, a dynamic element (specifying function f_x) under the impact of which the item unfolds. The other function, f_y, which is opposed to the first one, specifies (b) in its first occurrence. Thus, (b) is alternately specified by both functions, and thus can mediate opposites.

While analogy is specifically 'linear', Lévi-Strauss' formula is 'non-linear', *i.e.*, it implies a permutation of roles or functions and of terms, since (a), which is given as a term, becomes, once inverted, a^{-1}, a sign of function, and y, which is given as a sign of function, becomes (y), *i.e.*, a term which is the final outcome of the process. This permutation is necessary, according to our interpretation, to account for structural patterns in which the final result is not merely a cyclical return to the point of departure after the first force has been nullified but a helicoidal step, a new situation different from the initial one not only in that it nullifies it but also because it consists of a state which is more than a nullification of the initial.[22] In other words, if a given actor (a) is specified by a negative function f_x (and thus becomes a villain), and another one (b) by a positive function f_y (and thus becomes a hero), (b) is capable of assuming in turn also the negative function,[23] which process leads

[22] In Propp's and Dundes' terminology, the initial situation would be, *e.g.*, LACK or TASK, and the final, LACK LIQUIDATED or TASK ACCOMPLISHED; the precision which Lévi-Strauss' formula brings to this structure appears to us first in pointing out the role of a mediator as a necessary agent of the transformation of a given situation, and secondly, as a more refined analysis of each of the polar situations, the LACK, for instance, being now analyzed into function and term.

[23] The negative function of the mediator is his negative action against the negative force and is thus to be considered positive, that is, as specified by the same function as the first term, the mediator cancels out the first term's action. Gilbert Durant, *Les structures anthropologiques de l'imaginaire* (Paris, 1960), p. 215, sees the process as follows, "Arrêtons-nous donc sur ce si important processus d'inversion et demandons-nous par quel mécanisme psychologique se constitue l'euphémisme qui tend

to a 'victory' so much more complete that is proceeds from the 'ruin' of the term (a) and thus definitely establishes the positive value (y) of the final outcome. This time as a term, (y) is specified by a function which is the inverse of the first term. To put it metaphorically, the inverse of, say, a loss which expressed the actual impact of a negative power is not only a loss nullified or recuperation, but a gain so that $f_a{}^{-1}(y) > f_x(b)$.

Finally, it might be useful to point out that the two first members of the formula refer to the setting up of the conflict, the third to the turning point of the plot, while the last member refers to the final situation.

Another way of explicating our interpretation of Lévi-Strauss' formula is to point out that its three first members, $f_x(a)$, $f_y(b)$, and $f_x(b)$, express a dynamic process whose final outcome, expressed by the last member, $f_a{}^{-1}(y)$, is the result or a state, *i.e.*, the end of the process of mediation.

This process can be roughly described as an inversion of the initial state through the operation of (b), but as an inversion whose influence does not cease once it has been achieved. One can illustrate the process approximately thus :

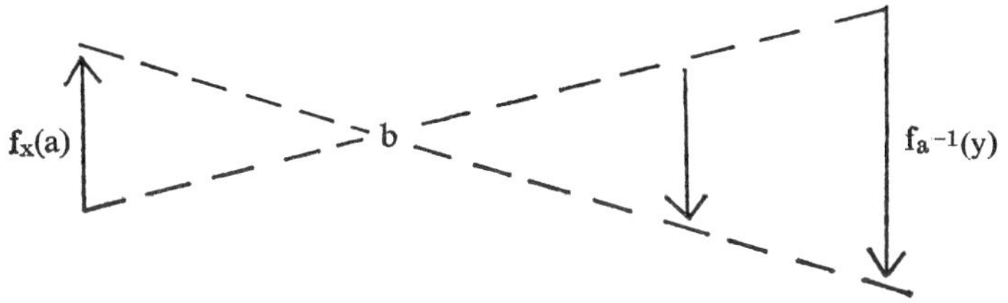

$f_x(a)$ b $f_a{}^{-1}(y)$

where (b), to use Lévi-Strauss' comparison, fulfills the function of a 'pinhole' so that the images seen through it become inverted and, if we may add, cast larger than life.

---

jusqu'à l'antiphrase même.... On pourrait définir une telle transformation euphémisante comme un processus de double négation. Processus dont nous avions rencontré les prodromes à propos de la dialectique du liage et du personnage du lieur lié. Processus que révèlent de nombreuses légendes et fabliaux populaires où l'on voit le voleur volé, le trompeur trompé, etc... et que signalent les centons à redoublement comme par exemple : 'Tel est pris qui croyait prendre...', 'A malin, malin et demi', etc.... Le procédé réside essentiellement en ce que par du négatif on reconstitue du positif, par une négation ou un acte négatif on détruit l'effet d'une première négativité. On peut dire que la source du rebroussement dialectique est dans ce procédé de la double négation vécue sur le plan des images avant d'être codifié par le formalisme grammatical. Ce procédé constitue une transmutation des valeurs : je lie le lieur, je tue la mort, j'utilise les propres armes de l'adversaire. Et par là même je sympathise avec le tout, ou une partie, du comportement de l'adversaire." — For a general view of the dramatic structure of plots, see *Id.*, *ibid.*, pp. 301-302.

In other words, if two opposite tendencies x and y in the opening of a folkloristic item actualize the deep opposition of two terms a and b so that a conflict, a 'problem', results, then the following operation (*) takes place

$$[f_x(b)] * [f_x(a)] \rightarrow f_a^{-1}(y).$$

This can be illustrated graphically:

$$f_x(a) : f_y(b) :: f_x(b) : f_{a^{-1}}(y)$$

Lévi-Strauss' formula borrows its symbolism from the alphabet of function theory but the connection with this mathematical field should not be carried further. He himself has never seen it as anything more than "a drawing" to illustrate the "double twist which is translated with respect to the passage from metaphors to metonymies and vice-versa" (personal communication, 1969).

The formula recurs as such only once in Lévi-Strauss' writings since its first presentation in 1955. In the second volume of *Mythologiques,* he concludes an investigation of a group of South American myths with the following words:

This passage from metaphor to metonymy (or the other way around), illustrated several times in the preceding pages and already mentioned in other works *(Le totémisme aujourd'hui; La pensée sauvage; Mythologiques I: Le cru et le cuit)* is typical of the way in which a series of transformations by inversion unfolds when intermediary steps are numerous enough. Consequently, even in this case, it is impossible that a true parity appears between the point of departure and the point of arrival except for the only inversion which generates the group: in equilibrium on one axis, the group manifests its disequilibrium on another axis. This constraint inherent in mythical thought saves its dynamism at the same time that it keeps it from reaching a truly stationary state. *De jure*, if not *de facto,* myths are not inert.

We thus find here an illustration in the form of a particular case of the canonical relation which we wrote as follows in 1955 [the formula is quoted].

It was suitable to quote it at least once in order that one be convinced that it has not ceased to guide us since.[24]

Lévi-Strauss adds (personal communication, 1969) that his references to Klein groups in *Mythologiques III: L'origine des manières de table* are the closest he came to the formula in his last book, especially in the

24 Lévi-Strauss, *Mythologiques II: Du miel aux cendres*, pp. 211-212.

following excerpt on which he commented by making the diagram reproduced below.

The mythological system of the bachelor brothers thus appears as four four-part structures mutually homologous and embedded. When one orders them in a logical manner, one can say that they articulate kinship links, behavior toward biological nature, behavior toward culture, and, finally, links between man and universe represented by the progress of seasons. But this embeddedness is not static. Far from being isolated each structure conceals a disequilibrium which cannot be balanced without resorting to a term borrowed from the adjacent structure. A diagram illustrating the whole configuration would be less like embedded squares than like a Greek fret: 'non-spouse' is not a kinship term; the inexistence of menstruation requires a leap from the physiological to the seasonal plane before it can express periodicity; the inverse of the end of a season is not equal to the beginning of another; and a sacrificial feast is not a profane meal fixed by an industrious cook. In the myths themselves, thought led by compelling dialectics raises from kinship to social functions, from biological to cosmic rhythm, from technical and economic tasks to gestures of religious life.[25]

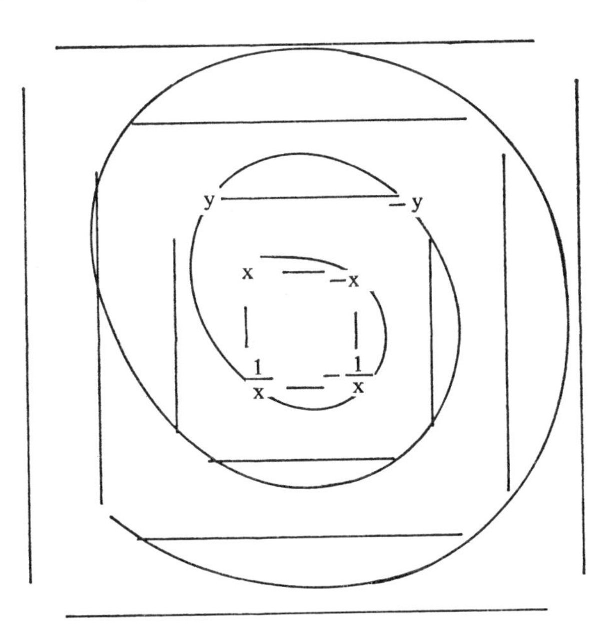

This helix is precisely the graphic representation of Lévi-Strauss' formula which we had proposed in the first edition of this monograph (Ch. 5, Model IV).

[25] Lévi-Strauss, *Mythologiques III: L'origine des manières de table*, pp. 294-295.

The formula, and Lévi-Strauss' theory of the structure of myths in general, implies a teleological view. In effect, myths are made to solve contradictions, according to this theory, and the formula can only be understood if it is read backwards, as the inversion of the first term, a in $f_x(a)$, becomes the verbal proposition which operates the substantification of the verbal proposition y in $f_y(b)$ to give $f_{a^{-1}}(y)$. Thus, a myth is built from its outcome — like a mystery story. The deep structure of a myth is the solution to a problem of a cognitive, sociological, technological, or other central order and, once found, it generates the myth in the codes available to the society.

1.2 OUR INTERPRETATION OF LÉVI-STRAUSS' FORMULA

1.2.1 *Application of the formula*

Lévi-Strauss uses his formula to account for the relationship between a whole series of variants of a myth[26] and the sociohistorical context from which they spring. As to the first point, a myth would then be the ensemble of not only all of its accessible variants, but also of all the variants of the counterpart of the myth with which one starts, although this latter aspect is not clearly stated by Lévi-Strauss; we think, nevertheless, it is an inescapable consequence of the interplay between sub- and superstructures he stresses so strongly.

We shall not enter into a discussion of this point here.[27] Suffice it to say that we have, on the one hand, broadened the application of the formula to describe different genres, and, on the other, restricted its application to arbitrarily selected variants; although a folkloristic item functionally speaking, in a given society, does not live alone but is interconnected with the complex body of some of its variants and with many others of different items, the complete series of the variants of a given item are nevertheless not to be found all in the same society.

Of course, our restricted application of Lévi-Strauss' formula leads to an approach entirely different from his. Lévi-Strauss' aim is to investigate the interplay of sub- and superstructures as it takes a place in the web of correlations between social and 'mythical' structures, while our purpose is only to point out some general recurrent patterns

[26] Myths, he says, are more clearly structured than folktales, and thus lend themselves more readily to structural analysis. "La structure et la forme", *passim*.
[27] This has by now been demonstrated by Lévi-Strauss' practice in *Mythologiques*.

of folkloristic items, and we do not want to enter into psychosocial or any other line of interpretation in this paper. Moreover, our strictly formal purpose would incur Lévi-Strauss' criticism since, according to him (*v.g.*, "La structure et la forme", *La pensée sauvage*), it is impossible to dissociate STRUCTURE from CONTENT. On the other hand, we are doing what Edmund R. Leach ("Lévi-Strauss in the Garden of Eden: An Examination of Some Recent Developments in the Analysis of Myth") contends wrongly that Lévi-Strauss does about the disentaglement of folkloristic items from the functionalist impact. However, we are not following in Leach's steps because: (1) we are not misinterpreting Lévi-Strauss but modifying his method to reach another end, when Leach distorts it to analyze data whose social context (and function) remain unknown; (2) our analyses remain exclusively on the formal level, contrary to Leach's — not to mention the confusion arising from the lack of critical investigation of the variants he uses, although such an investigation is required by the contentual nature of his study (*v.g.*, when he touches upon the kinds of problems the Biblical narratives try to solve).

1.2.2.0 *Units*

Parting from Lévi-Strauss' mythemes, gross constituent units, and bundles of relations as elementary units, we have used the more simple dichotomy of terms and functions which he himself sometimes uses similarly to Propp. Moreover, drawing from L. Tesnière and E. Richer, whose theory can be summarized approximately so that a grammatical function has to be discovered starting with the sentence as a whole, that it is an empty form which can be filled out by a certain number of interchangeable terms whatever they may be contentually speaking, we thus consider the structure as a matricial form and the content as a repertoire of sociohistorically conditioned terms capable of filling it.[28]

[28] Lucien Tesnière, *Éléments de syntaxe structurale* (Paris, 1959); Ernest Richer, "Un instrument de description formelle des langues: la théorie des lieux linguistiques", *Revue de l'Ass. Canadienne de Linguistique* VI: 3 (1961), 192-208; *Lieux linguistiques et latin classique* (Montreal, 1962). (Richer draws also from Hjelmslev, Togeby, Bally, Guiraud, Wagner, and Martinet.) "La fonction jouit d'une primauté absolue par rapport aux unités du langage.... La leçon à tirer de cette observation des faits, c'est que chaque unité de langage tire sa valeur propre des rapports structuraux qui existent entre diverses suites sonores présentes simultanément dans une seule et même phrase. D'où, le dictionnaire, pour être exhaustif, devrait nous avertir que *femme*, suite sonore française, appartient de droit à trois des traditionelles 'parties du discours': c'est un 'substantif' dans *il aime sa femme*, un 'adjectif' dans *une déléguée très femme*, et un 'adverbe' dans *réagir très femme*. Or, tous ces rapports entre suites sonores,

1.2.2.1 *Terms*

Terms are symbols, furnished by the sociohistorical context; the terms can be *dramatis personae*, magical agents, cosmographic features, *i.e.*, any subjects capable of acting, that is, taking roles.

The terms are mutually opposed in that those belonging to the category of (a) are univocal, while terms belonging to the category of (b) are ambiguous.

---

rapports constitutifs de la phrase elle-même, sont des ROLES GRAMMATICAUX.

"En conséquence, on voit que le phénomène linguistique se présente à nous très clairement sous l'aspect d'une immense totalité structurée dans laquelle un nombre variable de suites sonores reçoivent temporairement une fonction particulière, qu'on appelle un rôle grammatical. Le concours de tous les divers rôles grammaticaux édifie le système de la langue, et là réside en réalité le secret des communications rendues possibles entre les membres d'une communauté humaine." (E. Richer, *Lieux linguistiques*, pp. 30-31).

Similarly, but from a logical standpoint this time and following Wittgenstein, one can say that even the logical fact itself consists not of elements (or symbolic representations of things, propositions, etc.) but of the very OPERATIONS which bear on those elements, such as negation, implication, addition, multiplication, identification, etc.

Finally, an analogy with physics borrowed from a psychologist might help seeing how this approach of ours is not bound by contentual traits and can thus function in a cross-genres fashion. "Dynamic distributions are functional wholes. Take, for example, a simple electric circuit. The differences of potential and the densities of the current distribute themselves along the conductors in such a way that a steady or stationary state is established and maintained. No part of this distribution is self-sufficient; the characteristics of local flow depend throughout upon the fact that the process as a whole has assumed the steady distribution."

... "If all forces of a given dynamic distribution balance each other, their equilibrium will obviously not be disturbed if the intensity of all forces decreases or increases in the same proportion. Consequently, such dynamic states are largely independent of the absolute facts which obtain in their various parts. Assume, for instance, that the self-distribution is that of a current which flows through a conductor of a certain shape, such as an electrolyte which fills a vessel of this shape. The intensity of the current has no influence upon its distribution. Or also, if instead of ions like Na and Cl, K and Br or any others carry the electric charges, the distribution of the current is not changed. Or, take the electromotive phenomena which develop when two solutions ... of different ionic concentration are in contact. Such phenomena depend upon the RELATION of the ionic concentrations, while the absolute concentrations have no influence.... In other words, to be the electropositive side of such a physical system is a property which a part of the system owes to its position in the whole system". (Wolfgang Köhler, *Gestalt Psychology*, pp. 80, 119-120).

Thus, the "differences of potential and the densities of the current" (contentual characteristics) in such "dynamic distributions" as folkloristic structures would not disturb the kind of equilibrium proper to given types of those structures. I.e., whether the 'content' be cosmogonic (myths) or entertaining (märchen), etc., is FORMALLY IRRELEVANT, "if the intensity of all forces decrease or increase in the same proportion". And, "consequently, such dynamic states are largely independent of the absolute facts which obtain in their various parts.... The intensity of the current has no influence upon its distribution. Or also ..." etc.

The terms of a given narrative cannot be chosen arbitrarily, but are provided by the narrative itself. The first term can be found in the narrative by discovering the univocal element in its initial situation, *i.e.*, the situation before the solution of the crisis. The second term (mediator) can be found by discovering the ambiguous element in the situation before the solution of the crisis.

Terms consist of concrete embodiments, actualizations, while functions are more general and abstract expressions of conflicting forces.

Although Propp (Ch. VI of his monograph) strove to separate the levels of action and the "domains" of actors, he failed to be consistent in the last analysis. Witness the following circular definition : he proposes a class of actors called villains whose "sphere of action" is villainy, that is, a villain is an actor who commits villainy and villainy is the action of a villain; and similarly with donors and giving.

We have tentatively, especially Maranda in computerized studies, resorted to defining the main character of a narrative purely statistically — the main character is the one who is mentioned the greatest number of times.[29] In addition, European (and other) folktales usually stage an opponent and a number of actors who simply bring into relief, or make possible, the actions of the two; these can be named test-givers and, according to the actions of the hero (and the opponent) can become helpers or adversaries. But they are as a rule undefined because the motivation of their actions rests with the hero's fate, not with their own selves. Thus we are inclined to see two 'fronts' in a folktale and a host of actors who can become allies of one or the other.[30]

One can easily agree with Aristotle and Propp on the point that it is not actors that matter but actions. And one could probably find, in a statistical or other overall analysis of a corpus of narratives of one culture that all actors can be grouped according to their most common and consistent actions. That is, certain kinds of actors (youngest son or youngest daughter, Petit Jean, etc.) are bound for certain kinds of action and outcome. But the terms, their classification and placement into 'slots' in the narrative stock, in our opinion, is something that happens on the level of deep narrative structures, interconnected and part of the *weltanschauung* of the group, whereas the unfolding of the different functions is something on the level of the surface structures and constitutes the narrative line or plot. Seen in this fashion, the invariances

[29] Maranda, "Analyse qualitative et quantitative de mythes sur ordinateurs", in *Calcul et formalisation dans les sciences de l'homme* (Paris, 1968, pp. 82-84).
[30] Fischer, "The Sociopsychological Analysis of Folktales".

and variances of folktales both become structural, but on different levels, taking part of different kinds of structure, both, however, culture-bound.

1.2.2.2 *Functions*

Functions are roles held by symbols. They form the dynamic composition of underlying active strings which gives the terms their bearing, their impact. That is, if the terms are not determined by functions, they are only floating elements.[31] Moreover, functions do not exist independently, but only as expressed in terms which give them their concrete figure.

The initial pair of opposite functions are only tendencies; in the final outcome, one of them prevails definitely, thus becoming a term according to the permutation mentioned above (1.1). This obtains, however, only in narratives with a certain type of ending; for more precise statements on that point, see the distinction between our different models.

1.2.2.3 *The interplay of terms and functions*

Terms are variable; functions are constant. That is : in a given body of materials, terms which appear in one variant can be substituted for terms which appear in another, provided that they fulfill the same function (as already stated by Propp).[32]

1.2.2.4 *Summary of our analytic units*

Terms: (a) and (b), respectively members of two sets, A and B, forming paradigms defined by their respective typologies in given societies (*e.g.*, dragon, devil, witch, ogre, etc. in Indo-European traditions; turtle, octopus, shark, lizard in North Malaitan traditions).

Functions: x and y, complementary verbal propositions which specify the terms (a) and (b).

Thus, with x = evil in Indo-European traditions, A will be the set of evil actors so that $A = \{a_1, a_2, a_3 \ldots, a_n\}$ where, for example,

a_1 = dragon
a_2 = devil
a_3 = witch
a_4 = ogre.

[31] Aristotle had already pointed out in his *Poetics* that it is not the characters that matter in a tragedy but the situation, the plot, or structure of events.
[32] Functions might be compared to social elementary roles, *e.g.*, father, brother, while terms might be compared to the given individuals (ultimately and abstractly stated, men and women) which fulfill them.

Given one verbal proposition, the other one is defined correlatively. This is because the formula rests on the assumption of an equilibrium axiom in human cultures to the effect that a 'balance of power' is postulated and that an increase in strength on one side of the equilibrium equation must be compensated. Strength is measured in terms of political, magical, economic, affective and other powers; it is expressed by "greater than" (>) and "less than" (<) signs in our formalizations.

The different operations performed in different items present regularities which are described by our different models.

1.3 OUR CAUSE-EFFECT FORMULA

As such, the formula is also parallel to a much simpler scheme, based on a study by Köngäs.[33] The corresponding members of the formula would be: quasi solution: quasi result : : final solution: final result — where : and : : express two correlative causal series — to which we shall later refer using the following abbreviations:

QS : QR : : FS : FR.[34]

1.4 OUR MODELS

In the course of our work, we soon found that our modification of Lévi-Strauss' formula only suited a limited number of items, those in which the final outcome[35] expresses an increase rather than a simple

[33] "A Finnish Schwank Pattern: The Farmer-Servant Cycle of the Kuusisto Family", *Midwest Folklore* XI (1962), 197-211.

[34] Although independently developed, this scheme is corroborated by neurophysiological studies. See W.C. Halstead, "Thinking, Imagery and Memory", in J. Field *et al.* (eds.), *Handbook of Physiology, Section I: Neurophysiology*, Vol. III (Washington, 1960), p. 1669: "Thinking is a form of problem-solving behavior which involves the correlation and integration of critical events in time and space. It is characterized by (a) a period of preliminary exploration; (b) a pre-solution period of search; (c) a period of vicarious testing of tentative solution; (d) an act of closure and registry of a memory trace, and (e) appropriate action. The essential process of thinking is the bringing together or grouping of critical events in time and space. If we analyze the key terms in this proposition, it is apparent that the term 'critical events', so far as the brain is involved, is synonymous with information, with the technical restraints of information theory."

[35] Cf. Aristotle's *Poetics* on the differentiation of tragedies: "It is just to speak of tragedies as being the same or different in respect of plot above all else, those being the same which have the same tying and untying." (1456a, 5-10).

return to the initial state. Some items, although they show the initial opposition, do not even allude to the possibility of a mediating process, and in some cases the mediator is unsuccessful. On the basis of our materials, we arrive at the following set of models, presented in the order of increasing complexity.

Zero mediator (model I)
Failing mediator (model II)
Successful mediator : nullification of the initial impact (model III)
Successful mediator : permutation of the initial impact (model IV).

Another model could be proposed for still simpler structures. In the case of some incantations, songs, laments, and small children's 'narratives' (Sect. 8), for example, no contrast is stated (or a contrast is implicit, but no change in the state develops and no mediation is attempted). The item unfolds as repetitious expressions of a single state. We will not discuss further this "model 0".

The set of models can be represented by a tree structure which at once is also a decision model for the storyteller :

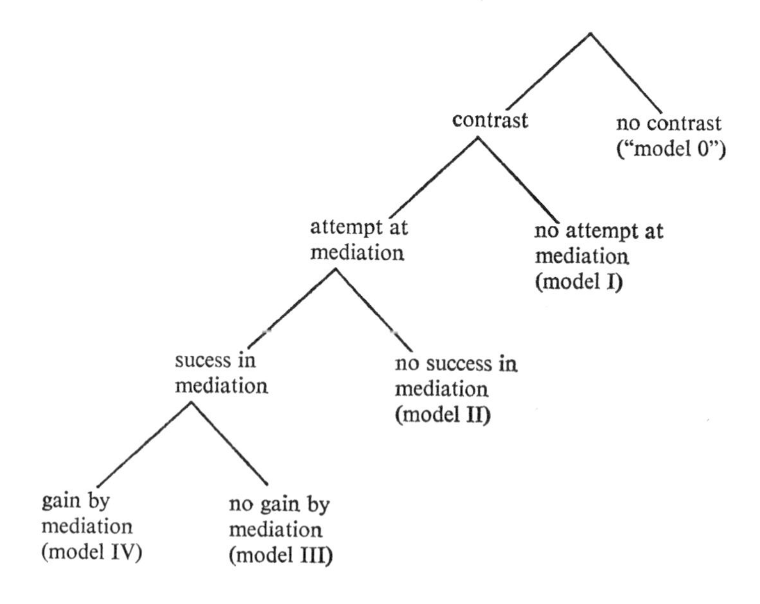

Our models are below presented by both diagrams and formulas. The visualizations by diagrams are complemented by attempts to provide more precise descriptions through the use of formulas. The signs + and – stand for what Osgood calls "valences" in his semantic analyses.[36] The division to 'positive' and 'negative' is not at all to be taken as a question of *Lebensanschauung,* although most of folkloristic materials provide us with such evaluations. Our division to + and – is simply given in the narrative in that they are TRUE OPPOSITES, sides which EXCLUDE EACH OTHER. Leaving cultural values and norms aside it is structurally the same whether love is expressed with a negative or positive sign, but it must be marked to be in an opposition to hatred; the same holds true in regards to the works of the devil, or any other contentual traits. That we follow the direction of marking destruction, hate, evil, condemnation, etc., with —, is only because it is clearer to follow the conventional division which is furnished by all materials and also immediately understood by our readers; not because we would confuse structure and such contentual aspects as values. This serves to remind us that mirror-picture structures are actually identical, which is also meant by our use of logical symbols such as A and $\bar{A}$ to state the same points on a more abstract level.

1.5 MATERIALS USED

We consider it necessary to test our hypothesis against genuine folkloristic items, before we pass judgment as to its validity. The selection of the test materials is arbitrary in that these narratives have not been pre-tested; on the other hand, we wanted to use good examples of each genre, the word *genre* taken here in the traditional sense. That is, all our materials can be found listed in standard collections of respective genres.

2.0 ZERO MEDIATOR (MODEL I)

In this chapter, we incidentally can use items which have already been structurally analyzed, namely a Cheremis sonnet, in conventional generic classification a recruiting song, discussed by Thomas A. Sebeok,[37]

[36] Osgood, "The Representational Model and Relevant Research Methods"; in Pool (ed.), *Trends in Content Analysis*; see also Pool, *Trends in Content Analysis*, pp. 218-223.
[37] Thomas A. Sebeok, "Decoding a Text: Levels and Aspects in a Cheremis Sonnet".

and a Finnish group of songs, sometimes classified as songs of repetition *(kertauslaulut)*, previously discussed by Matti Kuusi.[38]

2.1 LYRIC (SONNET)

The Cheremis sonnet runs as follows :

> Sky's cuckoo, my father, remains.
> Cuckoo wing, my mother, remains.
> Sky's swallow, my elder brother, remains.
> Swallow wing, my elder brother's wife, remains.
> Summer butterfly, my younger brother, remains.
> Butterfly wing, my younger sister, remains.
> Summer flower, myself, I depart.
> Flower blossom of mine remains.[39]

Sebeok's is a full analysis. Starting with phonemic observations, he finally reaches a level of investigation which is structural in the sense we use the word in this paper, *i.e.,* an investigation which pertains to the general pattern, the web of correlations which the composition constitutes finally. He summarizes his findings thus :

The song sounds one of the most conventional of romantic themes. The sestet pictures man and nature in harmony, the family circle and its environment coadunate. The images are symbols of order and stability : they are permanent, "remain". The envoy's preoccupation with the self is also in the romantic vein, "I", too, belong to the landscape, I am of nature, and have my proper place in my family. Yet must "I depart". But there is a seeming paradox here : the flower of summer passes away, but its blossom, its essence, "remains". Even so, the outward form of "myself" departs, but (the singer concludes) my essential inward being — my thoughts of you and your memory of me — stays here at home.

Upon a more elevated plane, the song is about death and its denial, immortality, a distillation of the same cultural experience as is epitomized by another instrument in the Cheremis folk repertoire, a proverb : "A man dies, his name remains"[40].

[38] Matti Kuusi, "Omaistenvertailukertaus", *Kalevalaseuran vuosikirja* XXXVIII (Helsinki, 1958), 89-108. This is one of the rare cases in which folkloristic items have been long classified according to their form; another obvious case would be formula tales. Kuusi states that these songs are known in Finnish and Estonian areas; additionally, we can find similar songs in, *e.g.*, Lithuanian folklore; see Jonas Balys, *Lietuviu dainos amerikeje* [*Lithuanian Folksongs in America*], (Boston, 1958), pp. 141-147; in which Balys gives the plots of seven different songs. Felix J. Oinas has recently established this pattern as Slavic.

[39] Sebeok, "Decoding a Text", p. 227.

[40] Sebeok, "Decoding a Text", p. 234.

Sebeok points out that "the images are symbols of order and stability : they are permanent, they remain". We want, however, to suggest the intrinsic opposition between all images and their correlatives respectively : the stable family members, *i.e.,* father, mother, older brother, sister-in-law, younger brother and sister, are all compared with flying, free-moving, beings (birds, butterflies, and, in the case of the women, their wings). Only ego's image is stable, namely a flower.[41] That is : other members of the family are compared with phenomena for which moving would not mean death; but the singer himself is compared with a being for which tearing off from its soil would mean death.

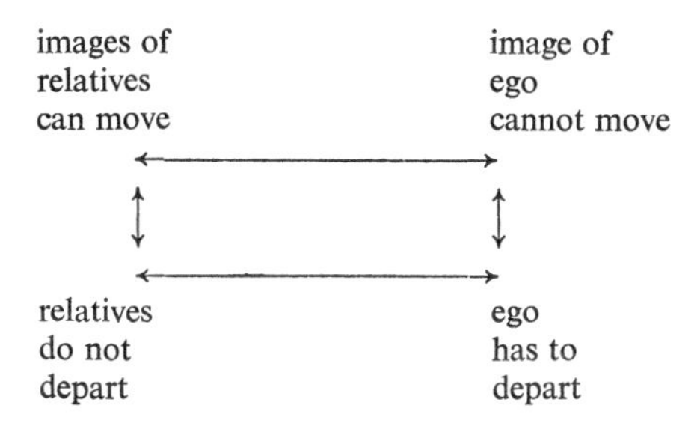

[41] Sebeok correctly points out the hierarchy implied in the imagery insofar that the female members of the family (metonymies) are considered subordinate of the respective male family members (metaphors); as to this series of 'totemistic' features, we note this suggestive passage : "Les tribus australiennes du fleuve Drysdale, au nord de Kimberley, divisent les relations de parenté, dont l'ensemble forme le 'corps' social, en 5 catégories nommées d'après une partie du corps ou un muscle.... Dans ce cas aussi, par conséquent, le système total des rapports sociaux, lui-même solidaire d'un système de l'univers, est projetable sur le plan anatomique.... On pourrait citer d'autres exemples, empruntés aussi bien à l'ancienne terminologie de parenté germanique qu'aux correspondances cosmologiques et anatomiques des indiens Pueblo et Navaho, et des noirs soudanais.

Il serait certainement instructif d'étudier dans le détail, et sur un nombre suffisant d'exemples, le mécanisme de cette particularisation homologique, dont le rapport général aux formes de classification que nous avons rencontrées jusqu'à présent ressort clairement de la dérivation :

Si

(groupe a) : (groupe b) : : (espèce ours) : (espèce aigle),

alors :

(membre x de a) : (membre y de b) : : (membre 1 d'ours) : (membre m d'aigle).

Les indications qu'on possède ... suggèrent que de nombreuses langues conçoivent une équivalence entre les parties du corps, sans égard à la diversité des ordres et des familles, parfois même des règnes, et que ce système d'équivalences est susceptible de très vastes extensions" (Lévi-Strauss refers then to Harrington, "Mollusca Among the American Indians", *Acta Americana* III : 4[1945]). (Lévi-Strauss, *La pensée sauvage*, pp. 223-224).

No mediation is sought in this sonnet. Thus, the idea of staying is only reviewed, when the line of staying relatives is inspected.

Sebeok maintains that the images of the sonnet express stability, and that they are structurally important in the poem. We maintain that the images of the sestet express freedom to move; but we question whether the images are to be seen as structural elements in the sonnet. They could be considered stylistic constituents, meant mainly to stress the deep tragedy of the hero's departure. What could be considered structural in their combination would be the following:

level of images	CAN MOVE		CANNOT MOVE
level of persons	STAYS	:	DEPARTS

That is, symbolizing 'motion' by M:
$^{M}/_{\bar{M}} > {}^{\bar{M}}/_{M}$, which, simplified, is $P > P$, that is a qualitative opposition between a given set and its complement; in more common words, a tension between two contradictory states which rules over the composition of the sonnet, without any attempt to mediate them — *i.e.*, with a zero mediator since, although the memory (or bride) remains, the hero himself nevertheless departs.
Leaving the images aside, the figure is the following:

−	+
ego	father mother older brother sister-in-law younger brother sister (ego's memory)

which can be expressed as follows:

−	+ + + + + +

or, in our final representation:

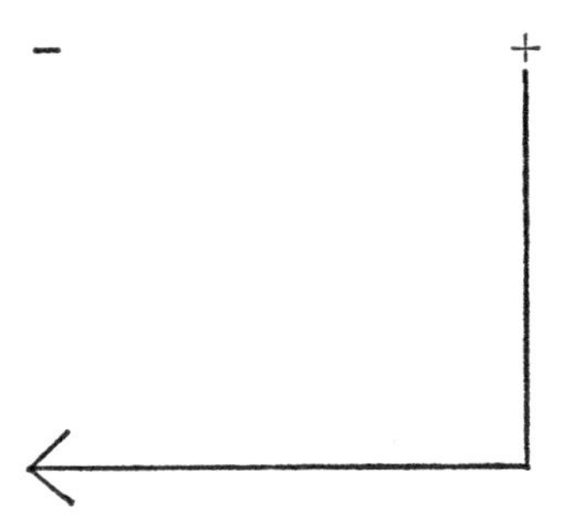

As a formula:

terms: a — ego
b — relatives $b_1 + b_2 + b_3 + b_4 + b_5 + b_6$

functions: x — departing
y — staying

$$f_x(a) > f_y(\sum_{i=1}^{6} b_i).$$

Reading: The departing function of the ego outweighs the staying function of the sum of his relatives.

We have named the sum as six, but if one 'answers the riddle' of line 8 with sweetheart, the number will change to seven. In this relation, the quantitative aspect of the summation — like the number of mediators in models II, III, and IV — is structurally irrelevant. The formula can be written:

$$f_x(a) \geqq f_y(b).$$

That the hero mentions his "blossom" which remains when he has to depart, can be understood as his almost rhetorical attempt to console himself and his relatives at the hour of departure. In Sebeok's interpretation "the outward form of 'myself' departs, but ... my essential inward being — my thoughts of you and your memory of me — stays here at home."[42]

The part of ego is not explicitly stated in the item itself. Following the logic of the sonnet, one would expect that the metonymic flower

42 Sebeok, "Decoding a Text", p. 234.

blossom is the female counterpart of the ego, i.e., his sweetheart, or bride, but this is also guessing. The analogy, or rather a string of analogies, consistently refers to women, through kinship or alliance, as metonymic parts of men, but leaves an open slot in the last line. This is presented exactly like a riddle :

cuckoo	: wing	: : father	: mother
swallow	: wing	: : elder brother	: elder brother's wife
butterfly	: wing	: : younger brother	: younger sister
flower	: blossom	: : myself	: X.

But the sonnet has still other, continuous analogies :

sky : cuckoo : : cuckoo : wing
sky : swallow : : swallow : wing

And changing 'domains' :

summer (earth?) : butterfly : : butterfly : wing
summer : flower : : flower : blossom

One could also tentatively suggest that these two domains, on which the hierarchical structure of the poem rests, sky/earth, group the men to married versus unmarried. This interpretation would swing the scale on the side of sweetheart instead of wife as the answer to the 'riddle'. Described using the cause-effect formula, this song is :

QS : "Free" relatives do not depart.
QR : No tragedy.
FS : Ego is bound to home but he has to depart.
FR : Tragedy.

The formula QS : QR : : FS : FR then reads : As the relatives who can move do not depart there is no tragedy in their lives (and indeed there would not be even if they did); but as the ego who actually cannot move has to depart, there is tragedy in his life (expressed the more sharply since it is contrasted with the lack of tragedy in the lives of the other family members).

2.2 LYRIC (SONG OF REPETITION)

A large group of Finnish songs, described briefly by Martti Haavio in his anthology *Kirjokansi*[43] and in detail by Matti Kuusi in his article

[43] Martti Haavio, *Kirjokansi* (Helsinki, 1952), pp. 229-232.

"Omaistenvertailukertaus",[44] fall into this category. Since the studies by Haavio and Kuusi do not give any variants in extenso, we quote our examples directly from the scholarly publication of Finnish folk poetry, *Suomen Kansan Vanhat Runot*.[45] We will use the standard abbreviation *SKVR*.

From *SKVR* XIII_1, we take two narrative songs, the structure of which yields model I. Both songs have been recorded in the same community, Sakkola, Southern Karelia, and they both tell about the same hero. *SKVR* XIII_1 18 runs:

1 Anterus left for war,
the tin-sheathed one left for battle,
the sheath of tin, the belt of silver,
the beard of golden curls,
5 the hair of golden locks,
the sword on his waist with mountings.
A message was sent to him:

Your father died at home.
How shall I dress your father?
With silken cloth and chamois leather.
How shall I make the coffin for father?
I shall have a silver coffin made,
the nails molded of copper.
How shall I take my father to the graveyard?
With his own stallion.

Anterus left for war,
[Lines 2-6 repeated.]

Your mother died at home.
How shall I dress your mother?
With silken cloth and linen cover.
How shall I make the coffin for mother?
I shall have a steel coffin made,
the nails molded of silver.
How shall I take my mother to the graveyard?
With her own gelding.

Anterus left for war,
[Lines 2-6 repeated.]

44 Matti Kuusi, "Omaistenvertailukertaus", pp. 89-108.
45 *Suomen Kansan Vanhat Runot*, 33 vols. (Helsinki, 1908-1948).

Your brother died at home.
How shall I dress the brother?
With a fine cloth.
How shall I make the coffin for my brother?
I shall have a silver coffin made,
the nails molded of steel.
How shall I take my brother to the graveyard?
With his own gelding.

Anterus left for war.
[Lines 2-6 repeated.]

Your sister died at home.
How shall I dress my sister?
How shall I cover her delicate skin?
Entirely with white.
How shall I make the coffin for sister?
I shall have a wooden coffin made.
How shall I have the nails made?
I shall have iron nails made.
How shall I take my sister to the graveyard?
With her own mare.

Anterus left for war.
[Lines 2-6 repeated.]

Now your miserable mate died.
How shall we dress her?
With rags.
How shall we have the coffin made?
Of a tanner's bark trough.
How shall I take her [to her grave]?
With a ram to the hill,
with a wether to the graveyard.

The hero receives five death messages, and his reaction shows his feeling about his relatives. His four blood relatives are worth the best care and most expensive equipment; they are contrasted with his "miserable mate" *(kurja kumppani)* who deserves the worst treatment. There is a similar hierarchy in the imagery as in the Cheremis sonnet, *i.e.*, the father is treated in the best possible fashion, and there is a descending scale of the images, the sister being treated most modestly, although still worthily.

The song is an illustration of a tense affinal relation — kinsmen are dearer to the hero than his wife. The figure is the following:

−	+
wife	father mother brother sister

which can be expressed thus :

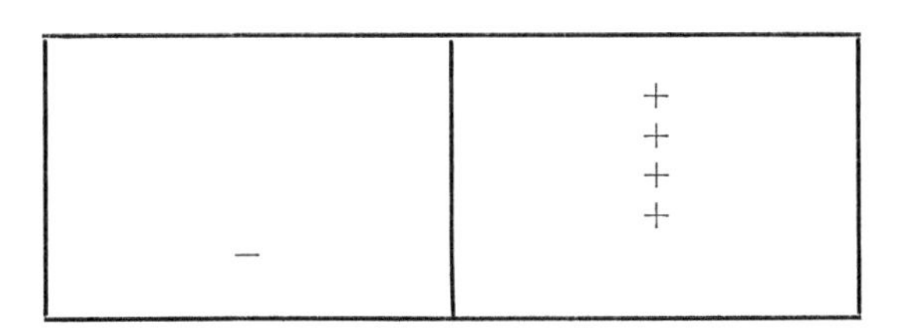

−	+ + + +

and again, in our final representation :

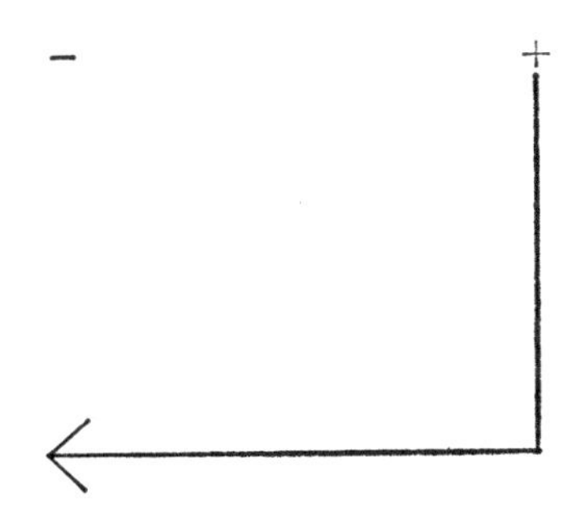

As a formula :

Terms :

a — spouse
b — blood relatives $b_1 + b_2 + b_3 + b_4$

Functions :

x — hatred
y — love

$$F_x(a) > F_y(\sum_{i=1}^{4} b_i).$$

Reading: The hero's indifference for his spouse is emphasized by his love for his blood relatives.[46]

We can again first present our cause-effect formula. Then we have:

QS : Blood relatives die.
QR : They are treated well, *i.e.,* buried in an honorable fashion.
FS : The spouse dies.
FR : Worst possible treatment, honorless burial.

QS : QR : : FS : FR then gives the following reading: If the death of the blood relatives is met with an honorable treatment from the part of the hero, then, in contrast, the death of his spouse is met with the worst possible treatment.

2.3 LYRIC (SONG OF REPETITION)

Our example of the Southern Karelian comparison of the relatives has its counterpart in a song recorded in the same community, Sakkola. In this variant, the following events take place:

Anterus leaves for war.

A message is brought to him: mother has died.

Anterus answers with indifference: if she died, it was her time to die; let the village *(miero)* bury her; fighting is more important for me.

Anterus leaves for war.

A message is brought to him: brother has died.

Anterus answers with indifference: if he died, it was his time to die; let the village bury him; fighting is more important for me.

Anterus leaves for war.

A message is brought to him: wife has died.

Anterus answers: now I have to go home, no more fighting for me. (*SKVR* XIII_1 19)

This variant is not as full as the previous one for not all family members appear in it. The basic structure is, however, similar to *SKVR* XIII_1 18, only contrasted with it in that now each relation is evaluated inversely.

[46] The English term "climax of relatives" which is used for songs of this structure, *e.g.*, Child 12, Child 13, and Child 95, in Francis James Child, *The English and Scottish Popular Ballads*, 5 vols. (1882-1898, reprinted in New York, 1956), is not appropriate, since no climax is to be observed, only an opposition between blood relatives and affinal partner. See also "Climax of Relations", in Maria Leach (ed.), *Standard Dictionary of Folklore, Mythology, and Legend, I* (New York, 1949), 236.

This means, above all, that the final outcome now is 'positive' as opposed to the 'negative' outcome of the previous song. As Kuusi has correctly pointed out, these songs each "declare the power of Eros", in other words : the topic of these songs is the person who is mentioned last and with whom all the others are contrasted.[47]

The structure of *SKVR* XIII_1 19 would be :

–	+
mother brother	wife

that is :

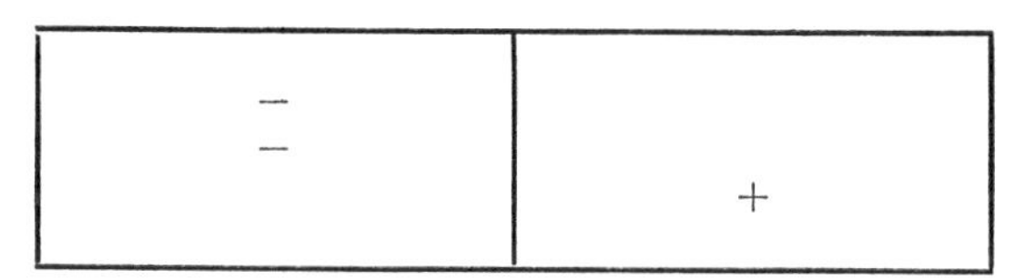

As a figure :

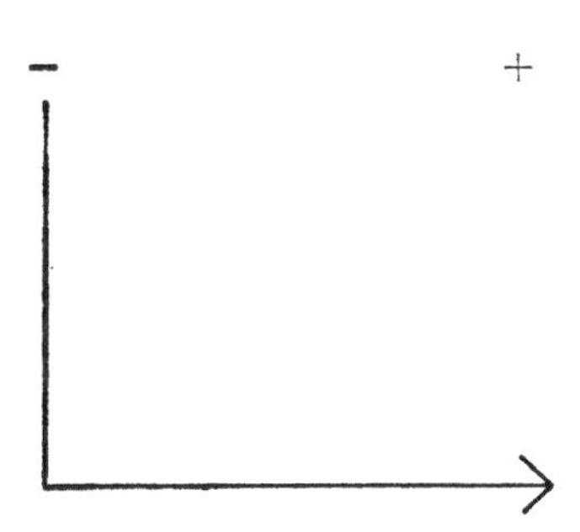

As a formula :

Terms :

a — spouse

b — blood relatives $b_2 + b_3$ (in the series $b_1, \dots, b_4$, above, 2.2)

Functions :

x — indifference

y — love

$$F_y(a) > F_x(\sum_{i=1}^{2} b_i).$$

47 Kuusi, "Omaistenvertailukertaus", p. 103.

Reading: The hero's love for his spouse is emphasized by his indifference for his blood relatives.

As the cause-effect formula we can express this song thus:

QS : Blood relatives die.
QR : The hero's indifference.
FS : The spouse dies.
FR : The hero's sorrowful reaction.

The formula QS : QR : : FS : FR then yields the following reading: If the death of the blood relatives causes an indifferent reaction of the hero, then, in contrast, the death of the spouse causes his sorrowful reaction.

Matti Kuusi reviews variants in which the series of relatives is full, *i.e.*, father, mother, brother, and sister, contrasted with wife; or blood relatives contrasted with the heroine's sweetheart or husband. He concludes:

> The method of comparison is simple: father, mother, brother, sister, and the erotic partner (bridegroom or bride, spouse, 'stranger') are in turns set to an identical situation: "Pay ransom for me, X!" "X died at home." "Is X treating you badly?" As to father, mother, brother, and sister, the result is expressed in identical or similar verses, as to the 'you' *(sinä)*, the result is in a sharp opposition. In twelve poems here described first, the relation between 'ego' and four close relatives is revealed as negative, the relation between the ego and his 'you' as positive; in nine cases described later, the result is contrary to this. The crucial point of the poems is, anyway, the fifth member: the 'you' is more important to me than other relatives, and I am more important to you than others are, whether the relation be hatred or love. The goodness or badness of four other relatives is given as a dark or light background, against which shy attraction or passionately black bitterness is pictured. ... In all their structural patterning, these poems declare the power of Eros more complexly than any other genre of Finnish folk epics, except the ballads.[48]

2.4 PRELIMINARY CONCLUSION

Thus, the models accounting for those two complementary types of cases, when compared the one to the other, are in the same logical relation as the two parts of the Cheremis sonnet studied above (3.1). In this present case, the songs, which are mirror pictures of each other,

[48] Kuusi, "Omaistenvertailukertaus", p. 103.

encompass the primary range of the emotional possibilities involved in alliance/consanguinity relationships, *i.e.*, love and hatred. Since our present purpose is only structural, we shall leave aside possible interpretations towards which structural analysis is a clarifying step.

A relevant interpretation should transcend mere psychoanalytical investigation, according to us, for psychoanalysis seems capable only of pointing out cases of complementarity without accounting for it; on the other hand, structural analysis provides a way of expressing complementarity as it obtains in given occurrences which are inclusive of psychoanalytical results, but the most decisive level of explanation should be looked for both in biology and logic.[49]

3.0 FAILING MEDIATOR (MODEL II)

Model II describes typically many myths made in the context of culture contact. In them, culture heroes fail in their attempts to endow their fellow men with technological innovations or new types of goods. The outcome is a restatement of the lack of those things which make white men powerful, and the myths are used to explain the disparity of technology or economy.

The following example might be interpreted as a case of successful mediation, if read from the point of view of the wronged man. But frequency analysis (see above 1.2.2.1) shows that the main *dramatis persona* is the judge (10 occurrences, including pronouns, against only one for the wronged man).

3.1 SAGE

In his standard collection of Finnish legends about the supernatural *(Myytillisiä tarinoita)*, Lauri Simonsuuri published the following *sage:*

There was a judge, who always passed a wrong sentence whenever he was given bribe. Once he had again passed a sentence against the law. The person who had to suffer without being guilty had wished that the devil take such

[49] "Toute explication psychologique finit tôt ou tard par s'appuyer sur la biologie ou sur la logique (ou sur la sociologie, mais celle-ci aboutit, elle aussi, à la même alternative) .... La logique formelle, ou logistique, constitue simplement l'axiomatique des états d'équilibre de la pensée, et la science réelle correspondant à cette axiomatique n'est autre que la psychologie." (Jean Piaget, *La psychologie de l'intelligence* [Paris, 1947], pp. 7-8).

a false judge. When the judge was then in the sauna taking a bath at midnight, it so happened that he tried to light his pipe, but the tinder-box dropped from his hand, and it was not found, however hard they looked for it. So the judge asked his servant to fetch another tinder-box. The servant went, but when he came back, the door was closed, and a groan was heard from the sauna. The door did not open, however hard they tried. Thus they went to fetch a priest, and the priest came, but he could not do anything for the door. Finally, when already twelve priests were behind the door, the door opened and the devil threw the skin of the judge on the beam to dry, but the judge he took with him.[50]

The main features of this legend are the following:

—	+
false judge	
false sentence	
wish that the devil	
take the judge	attempt to save the judge
	by 1-12 priests
the devil's victory	

That is :

—	+
—	
—	
—	
	+
	+
	+
	+
	+
	+
	+
	+
	+
	+
	+
	+
—	

[50] Lauri Simonsuuri, *Myytillisiä tarinoita* (Helsinki, 1947), p. 267; Lauri Simonsuuri, *Typen- und Motivverzeichnis der finnischen mythischen Sagen*, FFC No. 182 (Helsinki, 1961), E 266 and E 261.

As our final presentation :

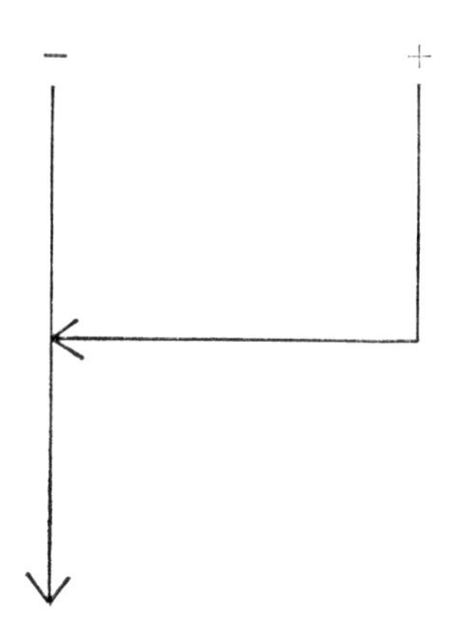

As a formula :

Terms :

a — unjust deed
b — mediator-priests

Functions :

x — damning
y — saving

$$F_x(a) > F_y(\sum_{i=1}^{12} b_i).$$

Reading : The damning function of injustice outweighs the saving function of mediators (priests).

Again, as the cause-effect formula :

QS : The judge passes a false sentence.
QR : An innocent man suffers.
FS : The wish that the devil take the judge.
FR : The bad deed is punished.

Which using the formula QS : QR : : FS : FR, gives the reading : If the judge's passing a false sentence results in an innocent man's suffering, then the wish that the judge be punished, *i.e.*, taken by the devil, results in the re-establishment of justice, *i.e.*, the bad deed being punished notwithstanding the mediator's efforts.

3.2 INTERCONNECTEDNESS OF DIFFERENT ASPECTS OF ONE ITEM

Practically, a narrative like this *sage*, which as such is a strongly moralistic warning *sage*, cannot be read isolated from its message; as we stated above, different aspects of a given item, *i.e.*, structural, functional, etc., are aspects of one item, and thus inseparably interwoven. That is, especially in this case (but equally so in the songs discussed above), the psychosocial function, the emotional value of the item, is embedded in the folkloristic structure. The aim of structural analysis is to mark how the content is organized and how the function is expressed, not to negate the existence of the function or the content.[51]

4.0 SUCCESSFUL MEDIATION: NULLIFICATION OF THE INITIAL IMPACT (MODEL III)

Here we have a cyclical structure which differs from the helicoidal structure of model IV. In items of type III, the action of the mediator brings the state of affairs back to the point of departure after having counteracted the action that set the plot into motion. In type IV, mediation not only nullifies the initial impact but exploits it to advantage: what gave the mediator its strength — the verbal proposition y in $f_y(b)$ — is hypostasized or substantified at the end. This implies the view that in such items a cultural value, y, is reinforced by a demonstration of its power. In effect, in addition to being able to match the impact of an adverse action, it can at the same time nullify it and, extracting more power from this very performance, increase its own cultural weight.

We diagram the difference between models III and IV as follows (cf. above, the helix in 1.1):

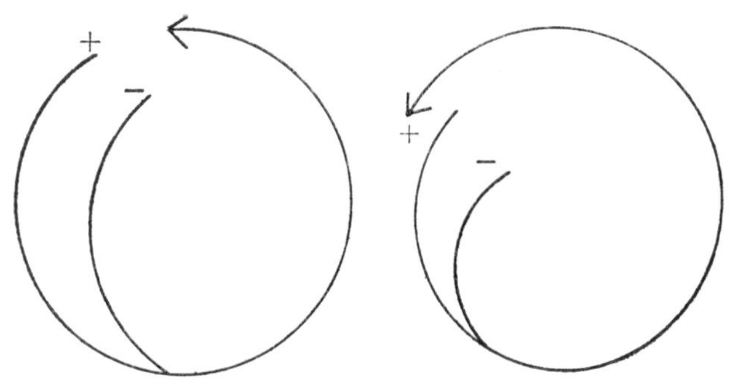

[51] See Chomsky's statement in footnote 2.

Or, in the way we usually present the graphic figures :

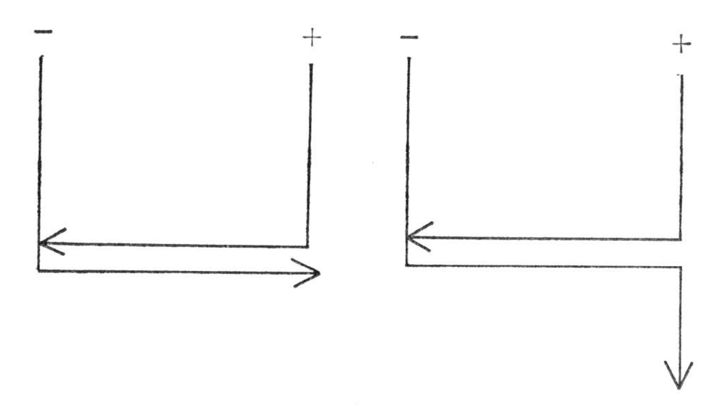

Here again we shall not specifically distinguish between positive and negative endings, since it is legitimate to treat models of positive endings as the inverse of those of negative endings, and vice versa.

4.1 SAGE

For the illustrations of the model III, we have taken narratives which are classified as belief tales *(mythische Sagen)*. The first *sage* runs as follows :

When they were driving nails to the coffin of the old woman of Soidinmäki, one of the nails happened to twist. Matti, the farmer, threw it to the nail box, and took another one. After this, the deceased started spooking. At night, it came through the door, like a human being. The door opened and closed, and one heard noise of walking on the floor. The ghost, who had a gray dress, went to the fireplace, sat down on a chair, put her feet to the stone of the fireplace, and warmed them up. Then it moved in the room as if taking care of something, rattled dishes on the table, went to the cupboard, and such things. When this had occurred on many nights, the maid Manta who slept in the room and always saw the ghost of the old woman told the thing to the farmer. The farmer mused : "She certainly misses the nail of the coffin which twisted and which I threw to the nail box." The farmer found the nail and drove it in the corpse-board,[52] and the spooking stopped at once.[53]

[52] *Ruumislauta* is the name of the board which is specially made for the deceased and later kept for similar cases.
[53] Simonsuuri, *Myytillisiä tarinoita*, p. 95; Simonsuuri C 436.

The structure of this *sage* is :

−	+
nail taken back spooking	nail given to the dead nail given back spooking stops

That is :

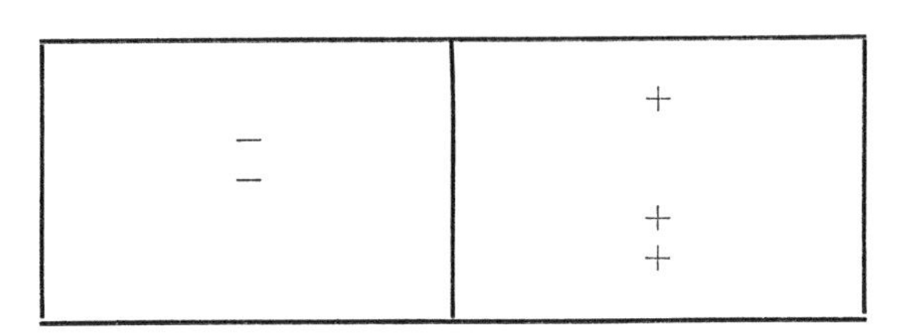

− −	+ + +

As a figure :

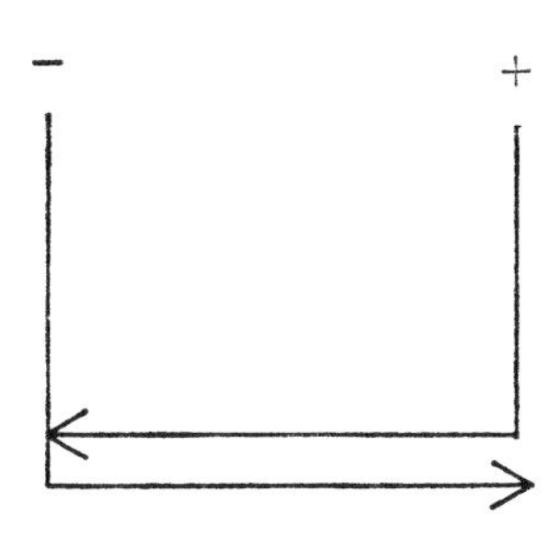

As a formula :

Terms :

a — (farmer's) 'theft'
b — ghost (*i.e.*, recently dead)

Functions :

x — disturbing
y — giving peace

$$f_x(a) : f_y(b) : : f_x(b) : f_y(\bar{a})$$

Reading : As the disturbing function of the 'theft' of the property of the recently dead disturbs the ghost, so the disturbing function of the ghost effects the return of the property (nullification of the theft) and re-establishment of peace.

Another way of 'drawing' the formula (see above, 1.1) would be, with * = "operation" :

$$f_y(b) \rightarrow [f_x(b) * f_x(a)] \rightarrow f_x(a) = 0$$

where it is the ambivalence of the term b which makes the operation possible.
As the cause-effect formula :

QS : A twisted nail (which was already given to the deceased) is taken from her.
QR : The deceased comes back to search for her 'property'.
FS : The twisted nail is given back.
FR : Spooking stops (*i.e.*, equilibrium).

QS : QR : : FS : FR.

Reading: If taking the 'property' of the deceased causes spooking, then giving back the property stops the spooking.

As pointed out above, this formula does not, however, describe the mediation process.

4.2 SAGE

Another case exemplifying our model III is another *sage* :

In Ylöjärvi, they had stolen a man's boots. The man went to visit a seer, the old man Tilli in Kuru. The old man asked him to bring brandy. The seer's own brandy would not help. Then the seer showed the picture of the thief in the liquor bottle. Additionally, he took a fresh bushbranch, made a knot out of it, and said : "In the course of three days, the thief will bring the ware back to you." On the third day, the thief rushed to bring back the thing so anxiously that he shouted already from a distance : "Where's Vältti? Where's Vältti?" The owner of the boots had a foreign name, but he was usually called Vältti.[54]

[54] Simonsuuri, *Myytillisiä tarinoita,* p. 181; Simonsuuri D 561 (D 691 and 701).

The structure of this *sage* is :

−	+
boots stolen	seer helping boots brought back

That is :

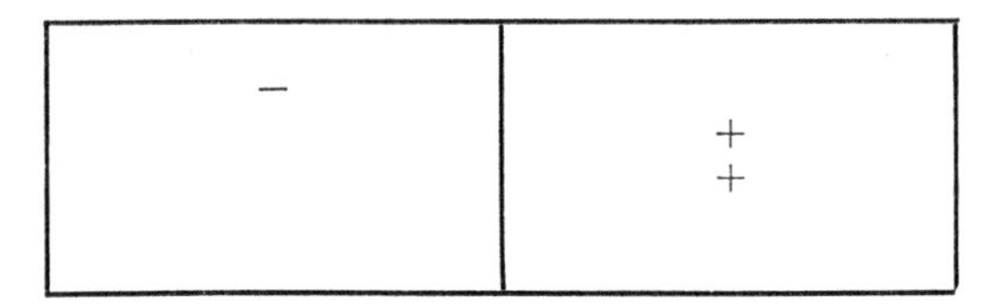

−	+ +

As a figure :

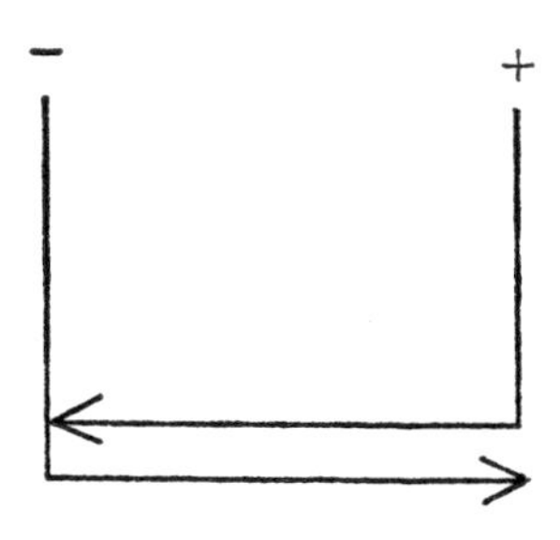

As a formula :

In this example, the mediator is evidently the seer, so that the final step would be :

Terms :
a — theft
b — seer

Functions :
x — harming
y — helping

$$f_x(a) : f_y(b) : : f_x(b) : f_y(\bar{a}).$$

Reading : The harming function of the theft is to the helping function of the seer as the harming (the theft) function of the seer is to the helping function of the nullified theft.

This type of ending, which consists of a mere nullification of the initial loss, or of a mere recuperation, is not of the same type as an ending implying increase. Actually, a permutative outcome implies that the final result is achieved through a nullification PLUS (or, better, nullification as a factor of) a 'gain'.
In the cause-effect frame:

QS : A man's boots are stolen.
QR : The man misses his boots.
FS : The seer reveals the identity of the thief and compels him to bring the boots back.
FR : The boots are brought back (equilibrium reestablished).

QS : QR : : FS : FR.

Reading: If theft results in the man's missing his boots, then the seer's help results in reestablished equilibrium.

4.3. MAGIC

4.3.0 *Charm as a part of the healing act*

The following Cheremis charm provides us with an interesting case which can be used as an exemplification of a holistic application of our binary analysis to magic action. The text is the following:

As the apple-tree blossoms forth, just so let this wound heal![All blossoms must be mentioned.]
When water can blossom forth, only then overcome me![55]

4.3.1 *Sebeok's analysis*

Sebeok's structural analysis can be summed up thus: the affirmative part of the charm, including the metalinguistic statement, which above

[55] Sebeok and Ingemann, *Cheremis: The Supernatural*, pp. 284-287. Following those authors' general line of interpretation in the first part of the following analysis, we shall consider this charm as an enunciation, which is prerequisite to logical formalization. But is it possible to leave its imperative value aside without distorting its very nature of charm? If not, the magician should then be essentially implied in it and we would have to take him into account (as mediator); see below.

appears in parentheses, is formalized with the help of symbolic logic. Thus :

$o \equiv$ blossoming tree
$o_1 \equiv$ blossoming apple-tree
$s \equiv$ imperative actor-action phrases,

so that $o \supset s$ expresses the structure of the first part of the charm, *i.e.*, "if o, then s" or "o implies s", which is a statement of "extremely probable opportunity".

Therefore the first part of the charm reads :

$$o_1 \supset s$$
$$o_2 \supset s$$
$$o_n \supset s, \text{ and, generally,}$$
$$O \supset S.$$

The negative part of the charm, *i.e.*, its last sentence, which expresses "extremely improbable opportunity", would correlatively read :

$$\bar{O} \supset \bar{S} \qquad \text{(non-O implies non-S)}$$

In Sebeok's words :

The entire first sentence can now be expressed in terms of a simple binary propositional operation, namely, implication, thus $o_1 \supset s$. With the use of an additional symbol, namely, a dot to express conjunction, the entire first immediate constituent, that is, the first and second sentences together can be expressed thus: $(o_1 \supset s) . (o_2 \supset s) . (o_3 \supset s) \ \ldots \ (o_n \supset s)$; but this is equivalent to (symbolized by $\equiv$) $(o_1 . o_2 . o_3 . \ \ldots \ o_n) \supset s$; and since $(o_1 \equiv O) . (o_2 \equiv O) . (o_3 \equiv O) \ \ldots \ (o_n \equiv O)$, and since, further, $s \equiv S$, we arrive at the expression $O \supset S$. The latter is regarded as equal by definition to the [first] sequence...

The internal structure of the actor-action phrase is the dependent clause of II., that is, ... "water can blossom forth" is very like the internal structure of the model phrase ... "the apple-tree blossoms forth" of I. The two phrases are not, however, absolutely identical. We must refer back at this point to the "motif of an extremely improbable eventuality" mentioned earlier in this paper. It will be observed that an assertion such as ... "the apple-tree blossoms forth" is true; that is, apple-trees do in fact blossom forth. Contrariwise, the assertion ... "water can blossom forth" is — within ordinary experience — false, that is, water does not in fact blossom forth. The verb ... "can" is the linguistic means whereby this difference in the truth-value of the two phrases is signalized. Let a superscript $^{-}$ represent the extreme improbability of such a fact as water blossoming forth. The phrase ... can therefore be symbolized by $\bar{o}$...

The entire last sentence can now be expressed in terms of the same operation — implication — as all the preceding sentences, thus: $\bar{o} \supset \bar{s}$.

Since $\bar{o} \equiv O$, and, further, $\bar{s} = S$, we arrive at the expression $O \supset S$. The latter is regarded as equal by definition to the [second] sequence.[56]

4.3.2 *A complementary analysis*

In a way, it may be said, as Sebeok does, that $\bar{o} \equiv O$ and $\bar{s} \equiv S$ (see below, this section). But $\bar{o} \supset \bar{s}$ cannot stand for the negative part of the charm because it can only mean, in the system of formalisation adopted, "When fruit trees shall not blossom forth, then do not heal." Now this suggests to see the charm as made of two explicit statements and two ellipses. It would then read, with the ellipses between square brackets :

> As the apple-tree blossoms forth, just so let this wound heal!
> [As the apple-tree does not blossom forth, just so let this wound not heal.]
> When water can blossom forth, only then overcome me!
> [When water cannot blossom forth, only then do not overcome me.]

We are therefore facing two statements which are not directly complementary, as Sebeok seems to believe, but only indirectly since neither the negative complement of the first part nor the positive complement of the second are given in the text. And it is through those ellipses that they find a strength of cohesion which is more striking than a mere redundant phrasing.

To illustrate this logical structure graphically :

First part and complementary ellipsis :

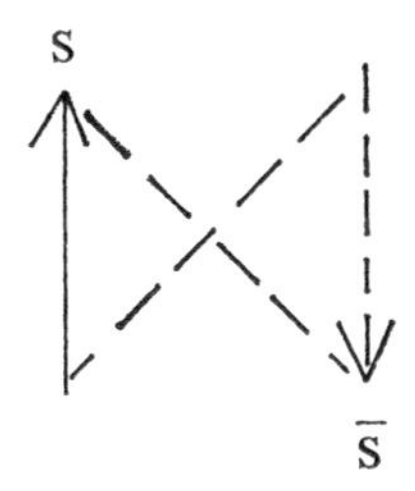

[56] Sebeok, "The Structure and Content of Cheremis Charms", pp. 382-383.

Second ellipsis and complementary part:

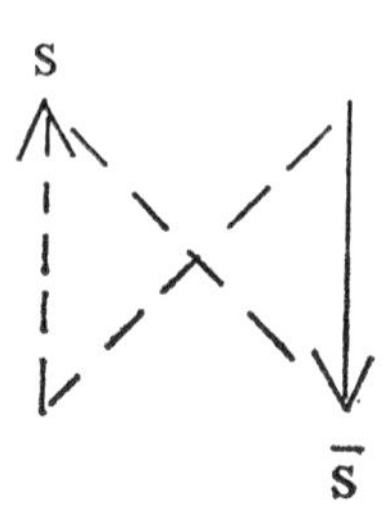

The completely explicit charm:

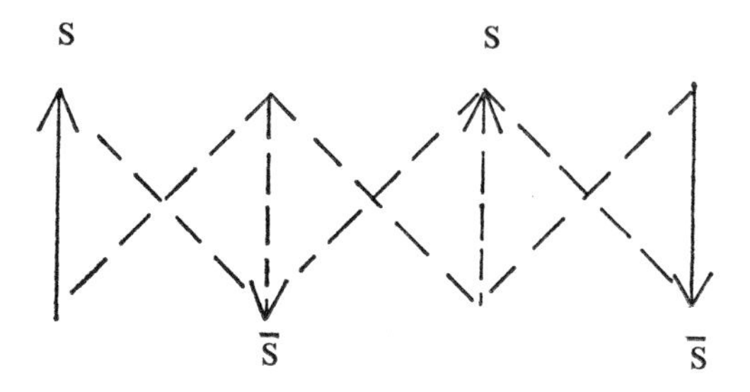

The charm as it stands:

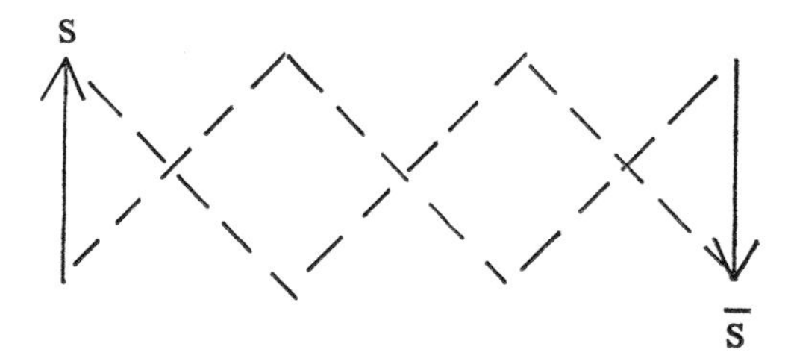

The first explicit statement can therefore be correctly formalized by $O \supset S$. As $\bar{o} \supset \bar{s}$ cannot represent the last verse, an additional symbol must be introduced to stand for "when water can blossom forth", and we will use p for that purpose. Then, let us agree with Sebeok that "overcome me" is equivalent to 'let this wound not heal', which is not necessarily so (see below, this section). We can now rewrite the formalization as:

$$O \supset S \quad \text{and} \quad P \supset \bar{S}$$

From which we see that $O \supset \bar{P}$, *i.e.*, that the charm rests on the cultural axiom that, with respect to blossoming, trees are in complementary distribution with water. Such complementary distributions could be investigated in the Cheremis corpus and the study should yield a restricted number of cultural parameters.

We see perhaps more clearly now that the charm stresses in two different ways the same positive ending and escapes from flat redundancy. Thus, starting from a positive statement ("as ... just so") it ends in the negation ("When ... only then") of a negative one ("Overcome me") whose function is to confirm the former. The relation established between two such complementary statements reinforces the one-way direction of this type of structure: it consists in (1) an affirmation, and (2) the negation of its inverse, so that the final design is unequivocal. Therefore, the process would not be a mediating one but a juxtaposition stressing a definite opposition whose one pole it nullifies implicitly.

If we compare this type of structure with the ones we exemplified in our model I, the result is as follows (see also 4.4). In our model I, we have a SINGLE SUBJECT of TWO OPPOSITE FUNCTIONS which he cannot mediate, *i.e.*, a singer wishing he could remain but having to depart or a singer's love and hatred; in the case of the charm, we have a SINGLE FUNCTION, S, emphasized by opposite statements one of which is impossible. Model I cases correspond to this figure:

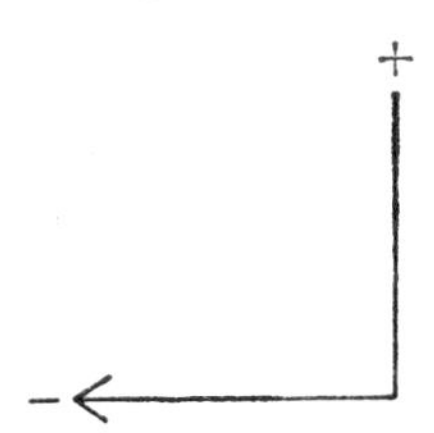

while the charm has to be represented this way:

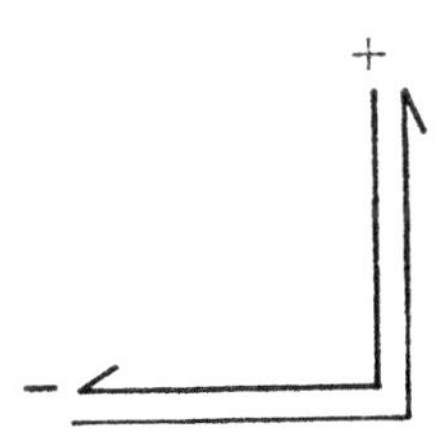

Model I cases end with an emphasis on one of the opposites; the charm, with an emphasis on the solution of the opposition to healing. But how does S, the solution, obtain in the latter? By virtue of the text itself which expresses the same thing in two opposed but finally convergent ways. Is that a mediating process or only double-affirmation? And if there is mediation, how does it obtain?

We suggested above (4.0) that there is a difference between an item which ends by a simple neutralization of an initial impact and an item which ends by an improvement over the initial state. In the case of the charm, is the outcome (healed wound) only a state of health regained or is it also something more than that, *viz.*, a reinforcement of the power the curer has over wounds (wounds can never overcome him)?

Should the first interpretation be given, the charm, interpreted this time as a mediating process through the magician, would then read as expressed by :

$$f_x(a) : f_y(b) :: f_x(b) : f_y(\bar{a});$$

otherwise, should the second interpretation be correct, it would read :

$$f_x(a) : f_y(b) :: f_x(b) : f_{a^{-1}}(y).$$

And the second interpretation contributes to seeing the charm along the lines of a theory of myth according to which model IV endings increase the social prestige of the mediator by substantifying it, as it were, through the exploitation (as a verbal proposition) of the very force to which he opposed his own powers (see above, 1.1). The middle term is thus the magician since he can perform both the healing and the conjuring, *i.e.*, first assume a 'positive' function (then reinforcing the magic blossoming-healing metaphor) and also assume a 'negative' function (then reinforcing the conjuration by nullifying the negative impact of the wound)

Reading of the formula :

Terms :

a — wound
b — healer (magician)

Functions :

x — spoiling
y — healing

$$f_x(a) : f_y(b) :: f_x(b) : f_{a^{-1}}(y), \text{ or } f_y(\bar{a})$$

Reading : The spoiling function of the wound is to the healing function of the magician as the spoiling (the wound) function of the magician is to $[f_{a^{-1}}(y)]$ forever nullifying-the-wound function of healing — or $[f_y(\bar{a})]$ to the healing function of the nullified wound.

We can, again, express the item as a formula without explicit reference to the mediating process in the following way:

QS : Healing incantation.
QR : Positive process going on.
FS : Conjuration.
FR : End of the process in the final state.

QS : QR : : FS : FR

In a simple reading, the first half of the formula refers to a normal state of nature in which equilibrium persists, *i.e.*, trees blossom and blood is not spilled; the second half refers to the improbability of an abnormal state of nature, in which the natural order would be upset, *e.g.*, water would blossom forth, and blood would be spilled until death.[57]

4.3.3 *Implications for the analysis of rituals*

The interpretation with reference to mediation brings forth an interesting problem as to the nature of charms as opposed to other folkloristic items. In our analysis, the mediator (healer) appears outside the text if we do not 'read him into the text' at the final point when he says: "only then overcome *me*." On the other hand, if we consider him as not furnished by the text itself, then we have to ask the question whether rites can be analyzed structurally only by taking into account their *Sitz im Leben*. This would conform to the definition of folklore we gave above (0.1 and 0.2).

Survivals, *i.e.*, relics whose living context cannot be known, could not be easily analyzed from the structural point of view, if our preceding formalization is correct. On the other hand, it might also be possible, when one has to start with a mere text, to achieve a reconstruction of the necessary context through structural analysis (as we did above, in a way).

In order to test this hypothesis, it would be necessary to analyze the same charm without reference to the magician as a mediator, as we

[57] Cf. Lauri Honko, "Luonnonjärjestyksen palauttamisen aate parannusriiteissä" [The Principle of the Restoration of the Cosmic Order in Healing Rites] in Pertti Virtaranta, Terho Itkonen, and Paavo Pulkkinen (eds.), *Verba Docent: Juhlakirja Lauri Hakulisen 60-vuotispäiväksi 6.10.1959* (Helsinki, 1959), 599-613: "The healer ... is the defender of orderliness [should be: order] and the restorer of the spiritual equilibrium of the community. ... both the psychological and the ideological, *i.e.*, mythical logic of healing rites can be depicted the same way. In both the restoration of the cosmic order is in question", pp. 612-613. Honko seems to presuppose that a myth is a necessary constituent of a healing rite; our example clearly shows that it is not necessarily needed, and still the 'text' used, the charm, works as myths do.

did after Sebeok (4.3.2). (Would this hypothesis bring charms to the category of lyrics?)[58] However, two major difficulties should be solved first: (1) Both the wound and the healing are given in the text so that it necessarily follows that the charm is used as a means of healing; in other words, its very nature is of a dynamic order, it consists essentially of a process whose final outcome is not to be found in it (as is the case in a narrative) but in the patient over whom it is 'spat', *i.e.,* chanted. Thus $f_y(\bar{a})$ or $f_a^{-1}(y)$ is to be found in the patient.[59] Structurally speaking, the text provides the negative and positive poles of the binary system as well as their juxtaposition; but the nullification of the negative term or its permutation to the role of function are only implicitly contained in the written document.

(2) The modes of the verbs in this charm give a clear indication of the imperative nature of the text. That is: it is a text composed to be chanted and thus necessarily implies a magician. In other words, in contrast to other narratives which are relatively complete in themselves, charms and rituals would, as normal 'text-recordings', not give sufficient information for analysis. This may appear too free a generalization, but one may perhaps suggest the distinction between narratives (*i.e., märchen, sage,* ballad and other epic songs) and charms in that the former group is 'historical' and 'objective' and relates a dramatic event without requiring a vital participation of either of the raconteur or the audience, whereas the latter is 'actual' and 'subjective' and makes both the performer and the audience participate in the dramatic act, the performer in an active, the audience at least in a passive way. That is, in other words: if we start, hypothetically, with an initial opposition, the difference between a narrative and a rite would be that the opposition in the former is solved beforehand, but in the latter, the situation itself

[58] Martti Haavio, *Laulupuu* (Helsinki, 1952), an anthology of Finnish folk lyrics, incidentally, gives a number of charm texts as lyrics. (Cf., *v.g.*, Lamartine's "Le Lac": "O temps, suspends ton vol...")

[59] Using Sebeok's model of folkloristic communication (here somewhat simplified):

↓——→ Code ←——↓
Encoder → Message → Decoder

in our analysis, we used the following elements:

Code
ENCODER → MESSAGE → DECODER

Sebeok's analysis does not detail any mediating process and thus perhaps treats implicitly such charms as lyrical apostrophes (see footnote 58). That kind of analysis is using only this part:

CODE
Encoder → Message → Decoder

provides the problem and the actor brings forth the solution, even if the solution is always expected to be the same (see 9.8), like in riddles.[60]

4.4 THE THREE FIRST MODELS

Before presenting our last model, it may be useful to review briefly the ground covered so far.

Model I consists of the juxtaposition of a relation A contrasting with its 'complement' $\bar{\dot{A}}$ (the quotation marks mean that it is not necessarily a true logical complement). It describes a single correlation, $A : \bar{\dot{A}}$.

Model II is of the same type, superficially, as model I. The important difference is that a relation A and its 'complement' $\bar{A}$ (which remains absent in the outcome) are brought together by the operation of a failing mediator, B. Model II therefore describes (1) a first correlation $A : \bar{A}$; (2) a second correlation, A : B; and (3) an ordered relation $A > B$, since $x > y$ in $f_x(a) : f_y(b)$.

Model III describes the same two correlations, $A : \bar{A}$ and A : B, but here the ordered relation is the inverse of the one in model II from the standpoint of the equilibrium of the forces in conflict, as we have $A < B$. In the outcome, $f_x(a) = 0$ because x is neutralized by y in the course of the action.

Finally, in model IV, as we shall see presently, the same two correlations are described as in models II and III. The ordered relation is the same as in model III, $A < B$. But the difference between model III and model IV comes from a "much greater than" relation between A and B, $A \ll B$, with the consequence that the power of B is hypostasized.

We summarize the description of our models with the help of the following simplifications:

Model I	$A : \bar{A}$
Model II	$A > B \rightarrow A$
Model III	$A < B \rightarrow \bar{A}$
Model IV	$A \ll B \rightarrow B$

60 Myth, as a text, would then be a narrative but more than the mere relating of it is needed to make a narrative myth : namely the actualization of the narrative in a problematic situation; this situation, its problem and solution, would then be psycho-socially equivalent to a rite. Cf. Lévi-Strauss, *La pensée sauvage*, pp. 313-323.

5.0 SUCCESSFUL MEDIATION: NULLIFICATION OF THE INITIAL IMPACT AS A MEANS OF INCREASING ON THE INITIAL STATE (MODEL IV)

For our model IV, which is the only unquestionable exemplification of Lévi-Strauss' formula, we have illustrations from different folkloristic genres, namely, *schwank*, myth, *sage*, and riddle.

5.1 SCHWANK

As to the genre of *schwänke,* we use a cycle previously studied by Köngäs.[61] All the variants of the cycle show a clearly uniform pattern; for this reason and in order to avoid repetitions, we discuss only two of them here. First, let us take Type 1560:

Well, once a farmer and his servant were starting their meal, as the neighbors were eating, too. So the farmer said that,

"Let's pretend eating, but not eat."

The servant contended himself with it, and then when they went to the field to mow, the servant took the blade off the scythe and said that, well,

"Now let's pretend mowing, but not mow."[62]

The structure of the item is:

–	+
farmer's trick servant's compliance	servant's counter-trick

That is:

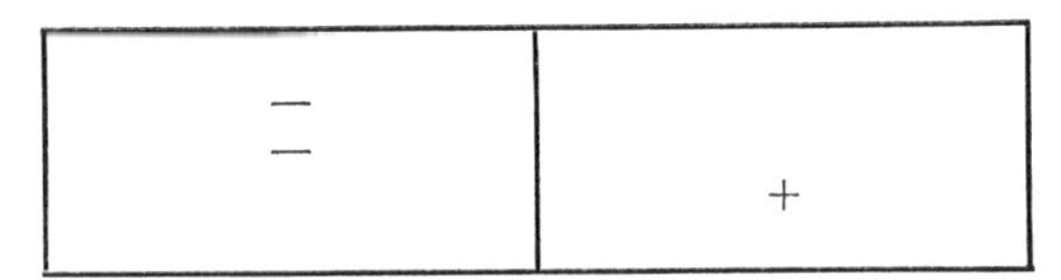

[61] Köngäs, "A Finnish Schwank Pattern", pp. 200-204. This pattern is said to consist of the following traits: setting/characters/problem/ quasi solution/ final solution/ message. Of these traits, characters are structural constituents in that they are used as terms; problem is stated implicitly in the setting, *i.e.*, the opening, as a prerequisite of the quasi solution. We have our clear structural units in quasi solution/ quasi result/ final solution/ final result (in the last, the message takes its definite place, as we will soon show).

[62] Köngäs, "A Finnish Schwank Pattern", p. 210.

As a figure:

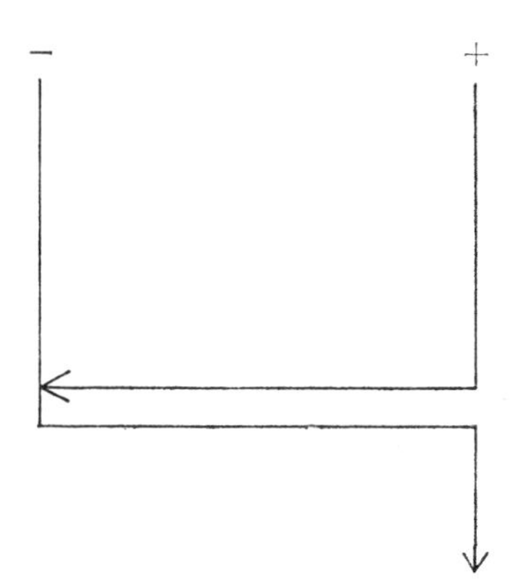

As a formula:

Terms:

a — authority
b — servant

Functions:

x — pretending
y — accepting pretence

The formula: $f_x(a) : f_y(b) :: f_x(b) : f_{a^{-1}}(y)$ then yields the following reading:

If pretending authority results in the servant's acceptance of pretense, then the servant's pretense results in the permutation of the authority function of accepting pretense.

Selecting the cause-effect units of the story as the basis for our analysis, we arrive at the following:

QS : The farmer cheating.
QR : The servant being cheated.
FS : The servant cheating.
FR : The farmer being 'paid back', and as a formula:

$$QS : QR :: FS : FR.$$

Reading: If the farmer's cheating results in the servant's being cheated, then the servant's cheating results in the farmer's being 'paid back'.

The interplay of structure and other aspects of a folkloristic item is clearly shown in our *schwank* because of its simplicity. As to why the *dramatis personae* of the story can as such be taken as terms, we must point out that these *schwänke* are in themselves already abstract insofar as the actors are not persons (with names, or personal characteristics), but only social roles, and that, too, only in opposition with each other. Furthermore, the initial opposition is given in the story without any other than the minimum of information as to the problem; if we mark pretended eating with P_1 and pretended work with P_2, we can retell the story, without changing it, in a form which as such is a structural schema. In other words, we have here a rare case in which a folkloristic item is built up with a minimum of content to cover the structural skeleton. It is also because of this simplicity that the psychosocial function of these *schwänke* is so obvious: it is, simply, that the master is 'paid back', beaten with his own arms; but since he is socially higher, his fall is greater than the servant's; the latter could not fall because he is already down. As to the style, it could be remarked, as an objection to Lévi-Strauss' statement that myth is the genre in connection with which the saying "*traduttore traditore*" loses its validity, that this very cycle of *schwänke* follows this principle better than any myth that one can find; and it is so easily translatable exactly because its content is reduced to a minimum and its style to the plainest possible, *i.e.*, because there is hardly anything but the basic structure in these *schwänke*.

5.2 SCHWANK

We take another example of the same cycle; this item is Type 1561:

Once a farmer and his servant were eating breakfast, and the farmer said that, "Could we at once eat so much that we will not need to come back for lunch?" And the servant was much ... "Well, let's eat. But wouldn't it be even better", the servant said, "if we eat supper at once, too, so that we won't need to worry during the whole day". Well, the farmer was very delighted with it, and then after they had eaten, the servant jumped to bed, and the farmer said that, "What do you mean now?" to the servant, and the servant said that, "Well, since we have eaten supper, shouldn't we go to bed?"[63]

It is easy to see that the structure is exactly the same as it is in the previous item; we can (and, in fact, must) state the constituents in an identical way.

[63] Köngäs, "A Finnish Schwank Pattern", pp. 205-206.

—	+
farmer's trick servant's compliance	servant's counter-trick farmer's compliance servant's humor

That is :

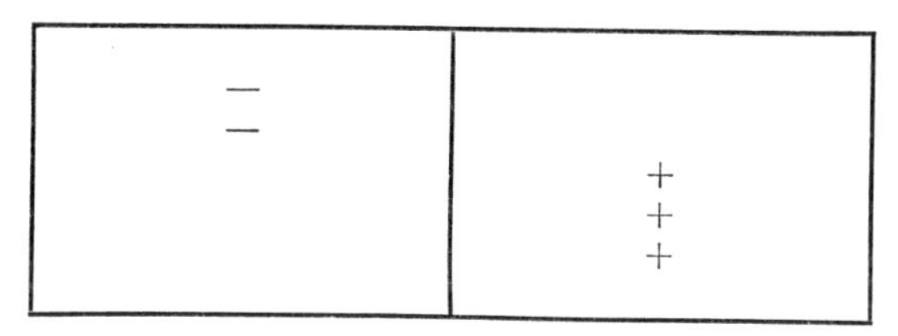

As a figure :

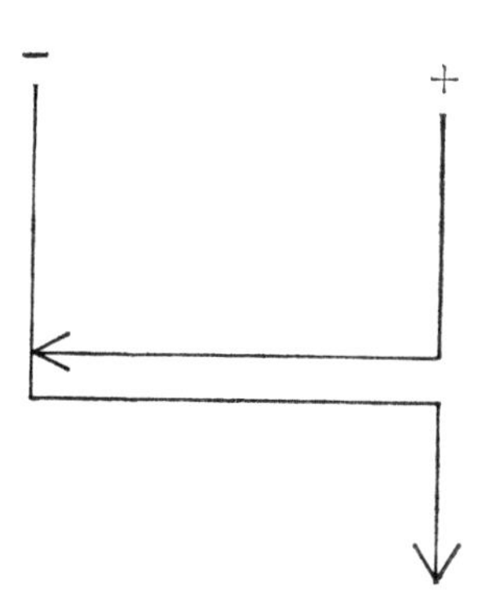

As to the Lévi-Strauss formula, we can phrase its terms and functions thus :

Terms :

a — authority
b — servant

Functions :

x — cheating
y — being cheated,

and the formula :

$$f_x(a) : f_y(b) :: f_x(a) : f_{a^{-1}}(y)$$

reads thus :

If the authority cheating results in the servant's being cheated, then the servant's cheating results in the permutation-of-authority function of the farmer's being cheated.
In the cause-effect frame :

QS : The farmer cheating.
QR : The servant being cheated.
FS : The servant cheating.
FR : The farmer being 'paid back'.

For the reading, see 5.1.

From the point of view of evaluating the formula used, it is significant that the final result is more than the mere denial of the quasi result, which would only be that the authority becomes the cheated one. In the actual final outcome of this *schwank*, there is namely an intrinsic message : the negation of authority, *i.e.*, authority based on social superiority. There is a shift of emphasis, the statement of the story that "the cheater is cheated and his status ruined". This is why more than a 'linear' formula is needed to express the emphasis of the elements of the narrative. And it is exactly here, in the last member of our formula, that we find the slot for the psychosocial function of the item, *i.e.*, $f_{a^{-1}}(y)$ which shows that even a servant can be superior to his superior by bringing him to an inferior position from which he cannot escape since he himself laid down the ground for the action, namely cheating.

5.3 SCHWÄNKE AND RIDDLES

The *schwänke* discussed above (5.1 and 5.2) and the cycle on the whole are narratives based on a problem. This problem can be stated in riddle form :

What is socially inferior and yet superior? — Intellectually superior.

We can, furthermore, form other, more specific riddles on the basis of this cycle thus :

Type 1560 : How can a servant pay back the farmer's trick of eating-pretense? — By working-pretense.

Type 1561 : How can the servant balance the situation when the farmer saves food and time by combining meals? — By combining meals further so as to reach the end of the working day.
1565** : How can the servant pay back if the farmer forces him to exaggerate the size of a fish? — By forcing the farmer to exaggerate the bestiality of a cat.
1567* : How can the servant complain about the lack of food? — By inventing a 'messenger'.
1568* : How can the servant get the piece of meat, when the farmer pretends he is turning the plate for the plate's sake? — By turning it farther, using the same pretense, until he reaches the piece.

If real riddles of this kind can be correlated to real narratives, then riddles and narratives are transformations of identical basic structures.

5.4 MYTH

As to establishing a good representative variant of the myth selected, Motif A 812, the Earth Diver, we used the summarizing article of Köngäs,[64] in which a number of variants are given in extenso and in which also the myth's essential constituents have been discussed. The following variant can be taken as one (but not the only) possible example :

> The whole earth was once covered with water, and there were no living creatures, save an eagle and a crow. There was a stump of a tree that projected above the surface of the watery expanse, and upon this the two birds were wont to stand and hold converse. Finally they became weary of the solitude, and between them they managed to create a duck, which swam about the stump. One day the duck dove to the bottom and brought up some earth on his bill. This struck the eagle and the crow as worth looking into, since they had never seen anything like it. They were very tired of having nothing but the stump to roost on, and as the mud brought up seemed promising, they entered into an agreement to keep the duck constantly employed diving for it. They could not agree, however, as to where the mud should be deposited. So they divided the world into two portions.[65]

The myth's essence has been aptly stated by Erminie Wheeler-Voegelin in the following manner :

> ... the culture hero has a succession of animals dive into the primeval waters or flood of waters, to secure bits of mud or sand from which the earth is to be formed.[66]

[64] "The Earth-Diver (Th.A 812)", *Ethnohistory* VII (1960), 151-180.
[65] Köngäs, "The Earth-Diver", p. 153.
[66] Erminie Wheeler-Voegelin, "Earth Diver", in Maria Leach (ed.), *Standard Dictionary of Folklore, Mythology, and Legend*, I (New York, 1949), 334.

—	+
water (not habitable = no earth)	creator helper earth

That is :

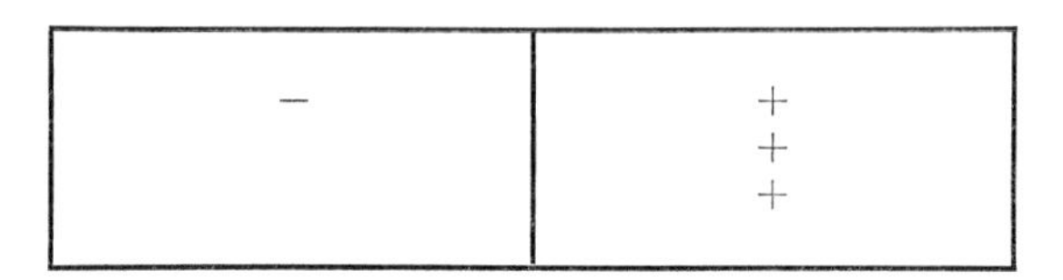

—	+
	+ + +

As a figure :

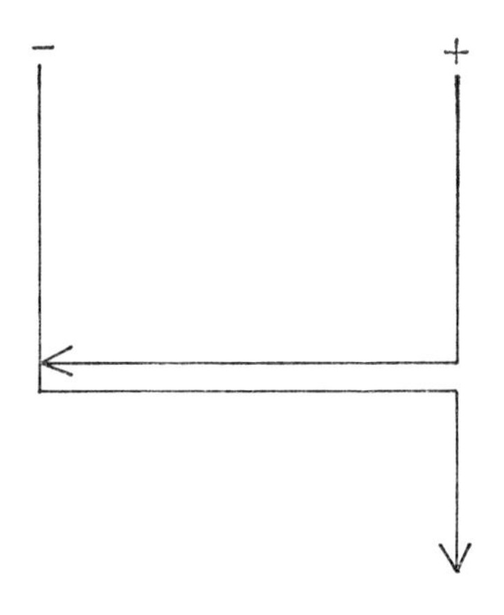

As a formula :

Terms :

a — water (almost universal)

b — the first being and his helper (*i.e.*, the 'non-diver' and the diver, who together form the creator)

Functions :

x — non-solid (non-habitability)

y — solid (habitability)

$$f_x(a) : f_y(b) : : f_x(b) : f_{a^{-1}}(y)$$

Reading : The non-solid function of practically universal water is to het solid function of the creator (capability of dwelling on water) as

the non-solid function of the creator (diving capacity) is to the permutation of water, which produces habitability.[67]
In the cause-effect frame :

QS : Water and the helperless first being.
QR : No earth created (the solitude, weariness etc. of the first being).
FS : Use of the Earth Diver, getting earth.
FR : Creation of the world.

Thus, the formula QS : QR : : FS : FR again expresses the initial situation of the narrative with its two first members; the third is the 'solution' of the narrative, *i.e.,* its turning point, and the last member of the formula expresses the outcome.

There, again, we see that the final outcome is more than a mere denial of the initial situation: in the beginning, there is only water (except the stump or other minimal support for the first being); at the end, however, there is both earth and water, and the latter is dominated in the sense that there is as much/little of it as the creator sees fit. The role of the mediator, in this myth, is to solve the initial insoluble problem of 'turning the bottom up'.

Again, we have the slot for the psychosocial function in the last member of the formula. More exactly : it can always be found in the last function. In the case of the Earth Diver myth, the psychosocial function of the narrative would be to explain how this world in its present order came into existence (by permutation of primeval water). In the case of the *schwänke* discussed above, which naturally are narratives of an entirely different kind, the slot is filled with a different message (the permutation of the social authority).

5.5 SAGE

The following *sage* is lengthy and repetitious, but nevertheless bears all marks of genuine storytelling; unnecessary to mention, this *sage* serves as a good example of how the length of a variant is a completely irrelevant aspect as to the structure.

67 If the capacity for diving is one aspect of the first being in our myth, we have in it a monotheistic creator concept; if diving capacity is attributed to the helper only (and creating capacity denied from him), we have a dualistic creator concept. See Köngäs, "The Earth Diver", pp. 167-169.

Once there was a poor woman. Her only cow got lost in the forest. The woman sought for the cow for the entire day, but did not find it. The next day, she started again looking for her lost cow, and she was very sad. The devil, in human guise, encountered the woman, and asked what had happened to her since she was so sorry. The woman replied that she had lost her cow and not found it anywhere. The devil said to the woman : "If you give what you have under your belt to me, after fifteen years, you will find your cow."

The woman touched her belt, and the key of the storehouse was [hanging] under it. She promised to give what she had under her belt, if only the cow would be found. The lost cow was found at once. The woman started driving it home. At home, she realized that the man had not asked for the key of the storehouse, but for the child that she would bear, since she was pregnant. She also realized that the man in question was not an ordinary man, but the devil.

After giving birth to the son, the woman turned very sad. She reared him until he was fifteen. The deadline approached. The son asked his mother why she was always weeping and worrying. The mother told her son that she had by mistake promised her son to the devil already before his birth. The boy asked his mother not to worry and left for the priest. After hearing the boy's story the priest said the matter was of serious nature, and asked the boy to come to him three days before the fifteenth birthday.

When the time had come, the boy went to the parsonage according to the order. The priest took the boy into the church in the evening, placed him to stand at the altar, gave the wine and the sacramental bread in his hand, and asked him to offer them to anyone who would come for him and exactly know the sacramental words.

Devils came by night to fetch the boy, but not knowing the agreed-on words, they could not take him along.

In the evening of the second day, the priest again took the boy to the church for the night, and arranged as on the previous night. All possible sorts of devils came to fetch the boy, but the boy did not leave since they did not know the words. In the morning, the priest came and took the boy away from the church. On the third night, the priest took the boy to the church and arranged in the same way as on the previous nights, and asked the boy to await until he himself would come to him.

Again devils of many forms came to fetch the boy. Even one who had the appearance of the boy's mother came and asked the boy but he did not leave. Finally the devil came in the guise of the priest, and started reading : "The body of our Lord ..." He left the Saviour's name off, by which the boy realized it was not the priest.

In the morning, the priest himself came to fetch the boy, and recited the needed words fully, by which the boy knew that it was the right priest, and he dared to leave the church. Then the boy went home, and the devil no more had power to take him.[68]

[68] Simonsuuri, *Myytillisiä tarinoita*, pp. 248-250; Simonsuuri E 551.

The structure of the *sage* can be described thus :

−	+
a poor woman loses her only property	
	the devil offers continuation of earthly life
but her child's soul is lost	
	the priest's help
	the boy is saved

That is :

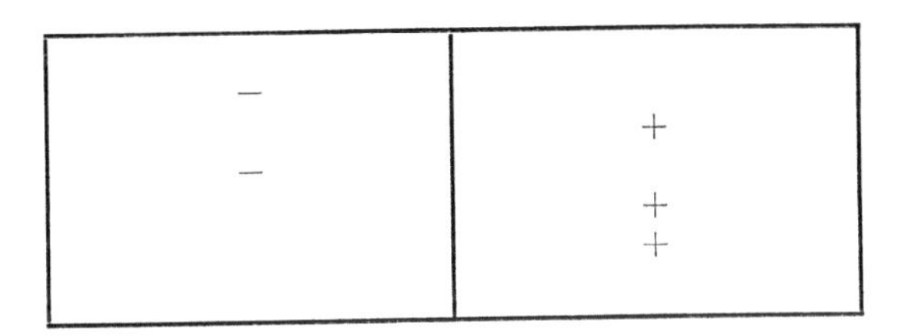

−	+
−	
	+
−	
	+
	+

As a figure :

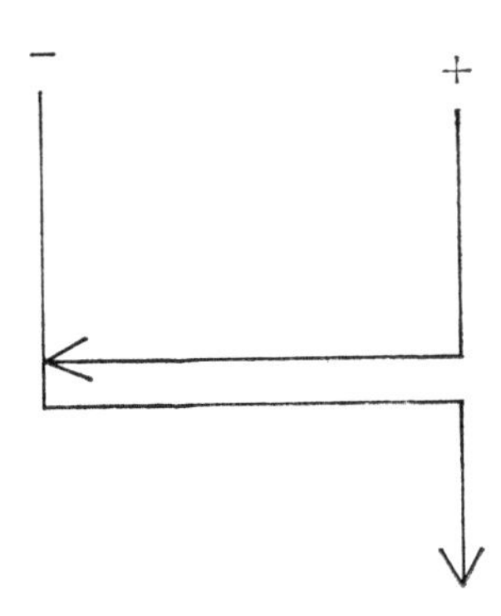

As a formula :

Terms :

a — the devil's power
b — God's power (represented by the priest)

Functions :

x — earthly life
y — eternal life

$$f_x(a) : f_y(b) :: f_x(b) : f_{a^{-1}}(y)$$

Reading: Seemingly, the devil's power helps the earthly life of man, and God functions only as to eternal life; but if man understands that God helps also in earthly life, the devil's power is denied and eternal life achieved.

In the cause-effect frame:

QS : The woman promises to give what she has under her apron.
QR : The lost cow is found; at the same time, it is realized that a soul was promised to the devil.
FS : The devil is kept from fetching the boy.
FR : Both the property is retained and the soul is saved.
QS : QR : : FS : FR, then reads:

The devil's help works for worldly gain, but for eternal loss; whereas God's help works for both worldly and eternal gain.

The mediator, in this narrative, is the priest; it is noteworthy that the priest uses religious objects as magic objects, and that this *sage* is practically identical with the *märchen* Type 330. It is of interest to observe how slight the distinction between different genres is and how completely, at least in certain cases, it depends on the psychosocial function. It is obvious that it does not matter structurally who fools the devil and by what means; but such things seem to be considered distinctive features when these stories are classified, so that we find the priest and religious objects (wine, bread) in the stories which are called *sagen*, and a 'secular' hero and his magic means (three wishes) in the stories which are called *märchen*.[69] In this special case, even the exact psychosocial function seems blurred; in the *sage*, there are certain magic traits, especially the use of the altar and religious objects; on the other hand, the *märchen* deals with the problem that the hero, *i.e.*, the smith, was promised to the devil and ends up in heaven, that is, his soul is saved, "and the devil no more had power to take him", to put it as it is put in the *sage*.

5.6 SAGE

Our next example of model IV is a mirror picture of the previous structures. The item, again, is a *sage*:

The servant of a farmhouse was given a very bad scythe when he was leaving

[69] See, for example, *Finlands svenska folkdiktning I A*, *Sagor*, vol. 1, (Helsingfors, 1917), pp. 134-140, Type 330, and Paul Delarue, *Le conte populaire français*, Vol. 1 (Paris, Maisonneuve, 1957), pp. 346-364.

for mowing. When he was mowing with it, it was difficult for him to cut hay with it, however industriously he whetted the scythe. Finally, before dinner, he lost his temper, threw the scythe on the fence and cursed : "A thousand devils may sharpen such a scythe, I don't bother any more", and he went home for dinner.

On the road men met him, walking as fast as they could, all with a half of a grindstone under their arm. He asked everyone : "Where are you going?" And everyone answered : "To grind, to grind, that the number should be full." The servant started feeling dubious as to the final outcome, since they were so many going to the meadow.

When the servant then had finished dinner, the scythe was on the fence well sharpened. When he mowed, the grass fell down so easily, at a wink. "Well, this is fine mowing", the servant thought by himself.

When he later, after a while, looked back, he discovered to his wonder that all the grass was standing, not one straw was cut. In amazement, he looked at his scythe, but there was nothing else left of it but the mere back, so had the grinders sharpened the scythe.[70]

The structure of the variant would be :

−	+
bad scythe cursing, i.e., calling the devil for help real work of the devils : the final state is worse than the initial	apparent help

That is :

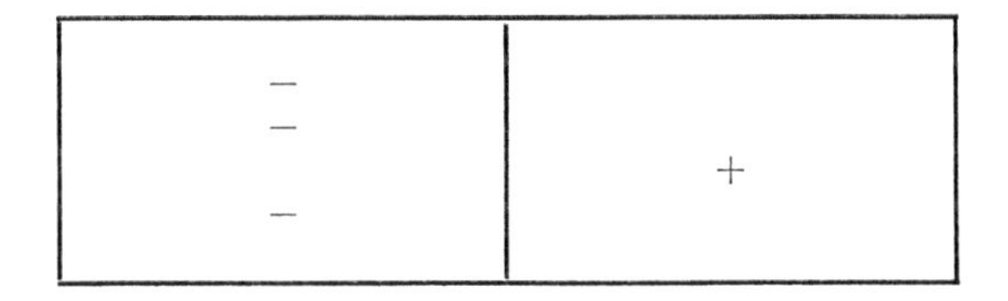

[70] Simonsuuri, *Myytillisiä tarinoita*, p. 276.

As a figure:

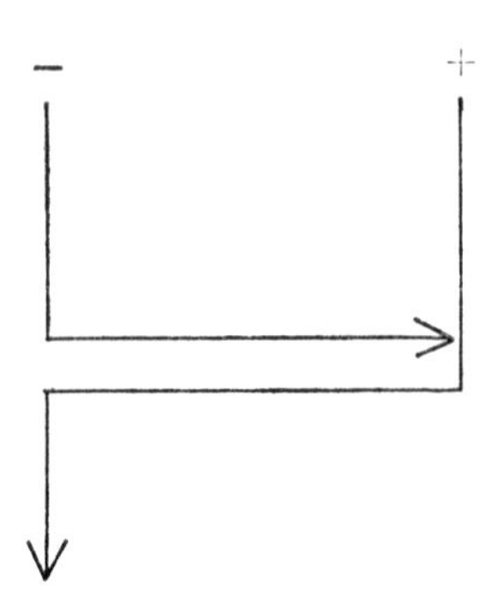

As a formula:

Terms:

a — scythe
b — devils

Functions:

x — inadequacy
y — deceptive help

And the formula $f_x(a) : f_y(b) :: f_x(b) : f_{a^{-1}}(y)$ then gives the reading: The inadequacy of the scythe is to the deceptive help from the devil as the inadequacy of the devil (as helper) to the ruined scythe in which deceptive help materializes. In oversimplification: the help of the devils brings forth the complete loss of the tool.
In the cause-effect frame:

QS : Calling the devils for help (cursing).
QR : The devils come to sharpen the scythe.
FS : The devils sharpen the scythe excessively.
FR : No work done, and the tool is spoiled.

The mediator in this *sage* is the "thousand devils" which, under the cover of helping, spoil the tool.

5.7 RIDDLE

Our next case will be a structural analysis of a riddle, to suggest the varied possibilities of our approach.

The riddle is:

What has eyes but cannot see?[71]

[71] Archer Taylor, *English Riddles from Oral Tradition* (Berkeley and Los Angeles, 1951), No. 277. Cf. 272-310, "A member normal in form, abnormal in function".

The riddle can be analyzed thus :

Terms :

a — eyes univocal (in the "normal", "literal" meaning)
b — eyes ambiguous (in any meaning)

Functions :

x — can see
y — cannot see

The formula $f_x(a) : f_y(b) :: f_x(b) : f_{a^{-1}}(y)$ then gives the following reading :

Univocal "eye" can see and ambiguous "eye" can not-see but ambiguous "eye" can see, with the result that the ambivalent meaning of "eye" validates "cannot see".

That is, if we take 'non-seeing' as the metaphorical function of eyes, then we see that the riddle image occupies the three first members of the formula, and that the last member gives the answer. Since the answer consists in the negation of the univocality of the concept, any answer which consists in metaphorical interpretation of the concept would be correct. In this case, one could follow the possible answers in different languages simply by observing what metaphorical meanings the word eye (and its translation) have. Such riddles seem to be truly international : *legs without walking (answer: table, bench, etc), ears without hearing (cooking pots, etc.), walking or running without legs (clock),* and so on, are met with in many countries; and it is always the possibilities of the language in question which provide the basis for such riddles. Our example, however, is not intended to solve the problem of the structure of all riddles, but only to point out that there are riddles which fit the structural formulas built to describe narratives. Such an observation — that different genres fit identical structures — deserves further investigation.

In the cause-effect frame :

QS : General first assumption : eyes see.
QR : No answer possible.
FS : There are other eyes than 'literal'.
FR : Answer : Metaphorical eyes, *i.e.,* the seeing function is denied as a necessary criterion for eyes.

The mediator, in this riddle, is evidently a concept of eyes which is capable of including both functions, which means eyes in a 'holistic' meaning, *i.e.,* in every possible sense.

6. PROVERBS

Finally, there are some proverbs which illustrate the simplest binary relational structure between terms and functions.

Alan Dundes has interestingly shown cases of what he terms EQUATIONAL PROVERBS which he formalizes: A = B. The following examples are taken from his paper but we are quoting them rearranging their order, *i.e.,* instead of giving them didactically, we present them simultaneously according to redundancy of terms and types of equation.[72]

I "Business is business"
"Enough is enough"
"Boys will be boys"

II "Coffee boiled is coffee spoiled"
"A friend in need is a friend indeed"
"The only good Indian is a dead Indian"

III "Seeing is believing"
....
"Time is money"

IV "Good hand, good hire"
"First come, first served"
"The sooner, the better"

....

V "Finders, keepers; losers, weepers"

VI "Service is no heritage"
"A fair exchange is no robbery"

VII "Half a loaf is better than no bread"
"Two heads are better than one"
"A taleteller is worse than a thief"
....
....

We would then formalize:

I as $x^A = x^A$
II as $x^A = y^A$
III and IV as $x^A = x^B$
V as $(x^A = y^A) + (y^{-1B} = z^B)$
VI as $x^A \neq x^B$
VII as $x^A \lessgtr y^B$

(where B can equal A, $_x$ and $_y$ then giving it its value).

[72] Alan Dundes, "Trends in Content Analysis: A Review Article", *Midwest Folklore* XII (1962), 31-38, especially pp. 37-38.

Thus, I and II and VII on the one hand, and III-VII on the other differ from the standpoint of term redundancy, and I, II-V, VI, and VII are four different types of equations. Disregarding this 'quantitative' aspect, the whole series can be represented by the non-specified relationship A/A', which is the most elementary relational structure.

7. SUPERSTITIONS

Alan Dundes, in his publication of Brown County, Indiana, superstitions[73] offers the following threefold classification of superstitions:

I. signs
II. magic
III. conversion

In his classification, the distinction between I and II is that "man is passive with regard to signs, but definitely active with regard to magic".[74] In other words, although both categories I and II consist of conditions and results, Dundes sees the distinction in that signs are not man-made, but magic is. Conversion, he says, is a procedure in which "sign superstitions are converted into magic superstitions".[75]

In the application of his three categories Dundes, however, fails to distinguish between voluntary action (which should be the only type included in his category II) and involuntary action, which, in fact, is equally passive as "the signs of the sky". Involuntary action, naturally, can be described as a means of producing signs by accident, without intention. That means that Dundes' category I is coherent and valid as his examples stand in the article,[76] but his category II erroneously includes many examples which are not magic at all, but signs thus belonging to his category I. Such are, for example, his numbers 68, 69, 71, 88, 100, etc.

It seems to us, however, that Dundes commits a more serious, *i.e.*, a theoretical, mistake in categorizing 'conversions' as an independent group. It would be better to express all three categories with one formula only, namely

If A, then B, unless C

[73] Alan Dundes, "Brown County Superstitions", pp. 25-56.
[74] Dundes, "Brown County Superstitions", p. 31.
[75] Dundes, "Brown County Superstitions", p. 32.
[76] Dundes, "Brown County Superstitions", pp. 34-39.

A would then be either a sign or a magic action, B its result, and C the counteractant used. If C appears as a zero, we have Dundes' categories I or II; if it has a value, we have his category III; but the difficulty of having either I or II as a presupposition, as a part of III, is then resolved.

This scheme can then be expressed with the cause-effect formula, thus :

QS : Condition (sign, etc.).
QR : Result.
FS : Counteraction.
FR : The result of the counteraction (good luck, etc.).

We will exemplify this with some actual superstitions taken at random from Dundes' collection :

Number 88. A woman with child should not see a snake, because it'll mark the child.

QS : A pregnant woman seeing a snake.
QR : The child will be marked.
FS : Avoiding seeing snakes.
FR : The child will be without (disfiguring) marks.

It is unnecessary to note that this superstition is based on a notion of a sign (involuntary seeing of snakes) which is to be avoided; that means that it belongs to Dundes' categories I and III rather than his category II where he placed it. In this, we have a sign and an action to avoid the sign.

Number 100 in Dundes' collection is a familiar sign superstition :

A four leaf clover brings good luck.

Now, we see at once that if we use our formulation "If A, then B, unless C", we must take C as zero; this is, by the way, intelligible, since this happens to be a good luck sign, and there thus is no need of changing the quasi result. Again, the item belongs to Dundes' category I, since a four leaf clover is a sign which cannot be made by man and which is also found when it is not looked for; but it is placed in the category II. In our formula, it is :

QS : Finding a four leaf clover.
QR : Good luck gained.
FS : $\varnothing$
FR : Quasi result remains valid.

Examples could easily be multiplied using only Dundes' collection; it would be very easy to show that all examples found in that collection of 219 items fit our QS : QR : : FS : FR formula, and, at the same time, our formulation if A, then B, unless C. We take the liberty of generalizing and assuming that these formulas describe all superstitions, since features like multiple conditions and zero counteractions are things to be considered features of content.

Furthermore, when $C \neq \varnothing$ but has a definite value, and then fulfils the role of a non-zero mediator, we would be facing a mediating process fitting our models III or IV. In fact, sometimes the 'conversion' is only a means of nullifying the initial impact (model III) as in Dundes Nos. 207 and 208, where "The two counteractants are both neutralizing conversion superstitions in that the proper action cancels the undesirable result" (p. 32). On the other hand, our model IV would account unequivocally for 'counteractants' which do "more than neutralize". "Another example of wishing as a conversion factor occurs in connection with the sign superstition : 'If you drop a comb, you'll be disappointed'. Stepping on the comb neutralizes this superstition but wishing changes a potentially maleficient situation into a beneficial one. 'If you drop a comb, step on it, make a wish and don't say a word until someone asks you a question'" (p. 33).

8. EXPERIMENTATION

In the course of the winter 1963-1964, under the auspices of the Harvard Center for Cognitive Studies, Köngäs Maranda experimented to establish the development of the mastering of different types of narrative structures in childhood. The subjects, between 6 and 12 years of age, were schoolchildren of Cambridge and Belmont, Mass. The narratives used were Anglo-American folktales of our types III and IV. To prevent the subjects memorizing the plots by rote, the texts were long : if it is impossible to remember word by word, the reteller must master the rules of the composition in order to arrive at a well-told tale. The narratives were in one experiment read directly to each subject in a face-to-face situation, and the child then repeated the story as he had understood it. In another experiment, tales were told to child 1, who retold to child 2 who retold to child 3, etc. All renderings, including the experimenter's, were tape-recorded.

Some very clear results emerged. The mastering of complex structures

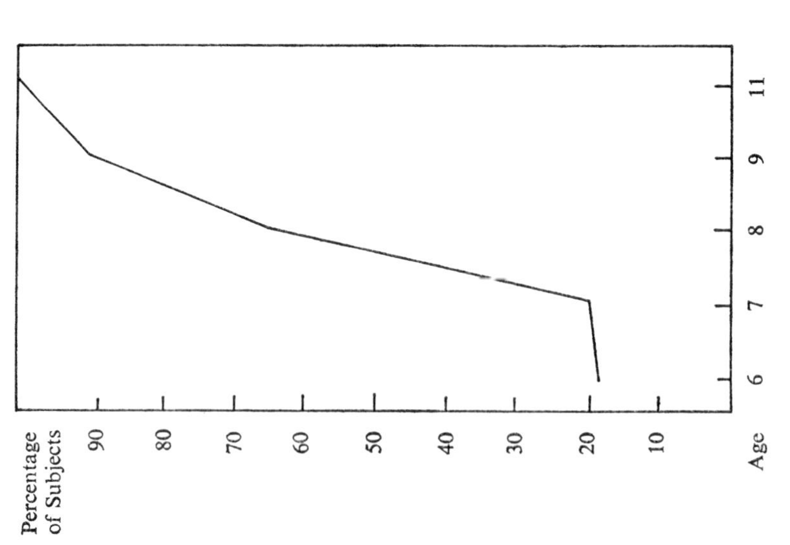

Overall conservation of structures (initial situation, mediation, and outcome) as varying with age.

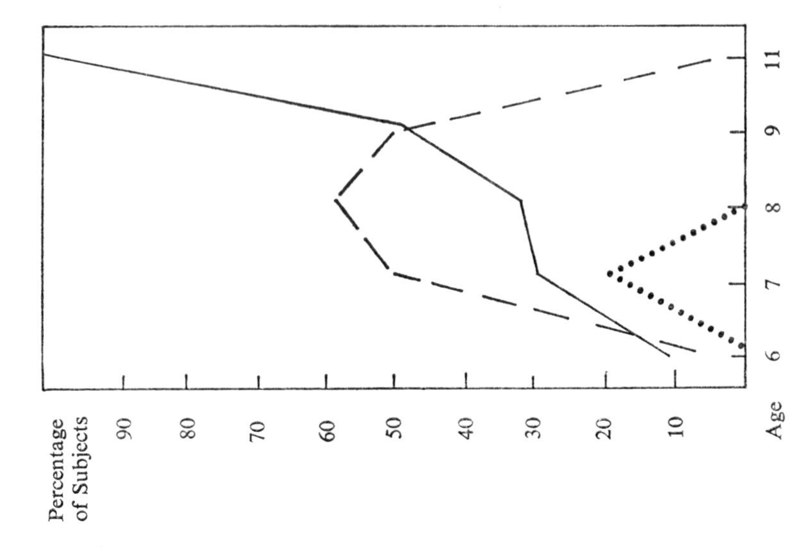

Initial situation : variation of conservation with age; fully conserved: plain line; partly conserved: broken line; reduced to a simpler pair of opposites: dotted line.

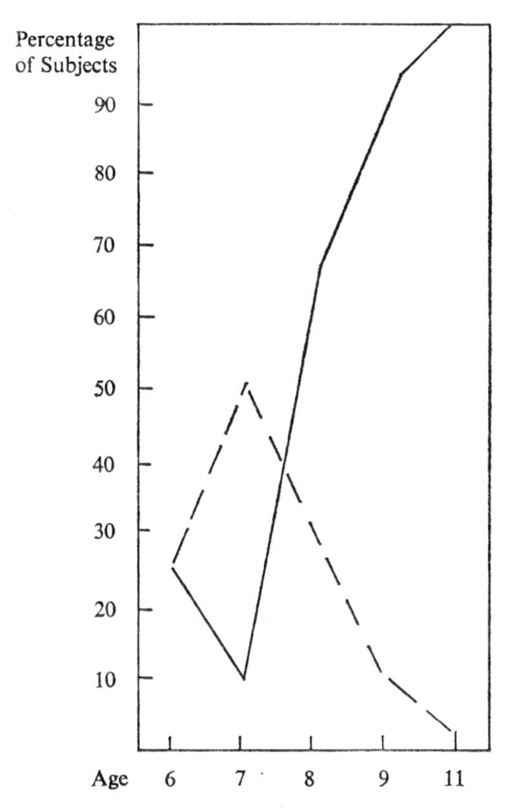

Outcome: variation of conservation with age; fully conserved: plain line; partly conserved: broken line.

was slowly achieved in this way: that the youngest subjects (6-year olds) either broke the narratives into incoherent fragments or reduced them to a contradictory structure; most of the 8-year olds simplified model IV to III or even II or I, and most of the 9-year olds and all older than that were able to conserve the structure in question.

Of course the age at which different kinds of structures are definitely mastered can vary from culture to culture, socio-economic class to another, and so forth; it may also be that children who cannot master a structure when it is 'concealed' in a lengthy narrative would master it in a short version. We find such differences of lesser interest at his point, and emphasize the finding that the complexity of structures corresponds with cognitive development. Thus our tree diagram (above, 1.4) contains the hierarchy of structures as a decision model which at least roughly describes the process of storybuilding. In a fashion, each simple structure is an incomplete complex structure, and in the developmental process during which a child gains competence the simple structures are mastered first and the most complex last, until the learner is in full command of narrative combinatorics.

9.0 CONCLUSIONS

Our discussion is for several practical reasons far from being exhaustive. We were not able, for example, since the space is limited, to test each of the models we developed against a large number of folkloristic items. Thus, necessarily, many of our statements appear as broad generalizations; the best way of evaluating them is to test them against more and more items of genuine folklore. They may stand the test; it may also be found necessary to establish more models, or perhaps combine some of our different models.

So far we wish to summarize our findings in the following manner:

9.1 *Use of recordings*

If the text itself, *i.e.,* the archived recording is used as the basis of a structural study, errors will take place, or, rather, the task will sometimes seem impossible, namely in cases in which the encoder and the decoder are part of the 'drama', *i.e.,* participate in the outcome of the item.

9.2 + *and* —

It is important to distinguish between structure and content, function, and style throughout the investigation. Even if it is, for the sake of convenience, to be recommended that socio-historically 'positive' phenomena be marked with the sign +, it is to be borne in mind that this sign marks only the contrast of what is marked with the sign —, and indicates nothing about values or norms. Thus, structurally speaking, such powers as that of the devil, or such acts as cheating could well be marked with +, if only their opposite powers and acts be marked with —.

9.3 *Mirror picture structures*

It is exactly because such opposition is purely a relationship that mirror-picture structures are in fact identical.

9.4 *Initial binary oppositions*

Thus, all folkloristic items which we have used, are structurally identical as to their openings, *i.e.,* we find an initial opposition in each of them.

9.5 *Mediation*

In some cases, the beginning is different from the end (models III and IV); in other cases (model II), it remains the same but after a vain attempt at modifying the course of action described in the plot. We call 'mediator' the especially fitted agent which insures the passage from an initial state to a different final outcome. Mediators are important cultural indicators. Comparisons of actors capable of fulfilling this function are significant both within broad culture areas as well as cross-culturally.

The distribution and predominance of some models in given corpora is also a point worth investigating. Model IV doubtless prevails in European folklore and probably also in other optimistic, 'winning', and rich societies. There, lowly heroes start from poor conditions of life and rise, in a 'capitalistic' way, to positions of wealth and high social status. In this respect, the conception of after-life is much greedier in European than in Eskimo folklore: in the latter, adequate means of subsistence are enough to bring happiness.[77]

We have observed that non-literate societies that were also winning cultures in terms of their own environments before contact and expressed the fact in many model IV myths are now in the process, in their acculturation myths, to shift to model II. Thus, the Gê of Central Brazil deal competently with nature. When they face the overpowering European technology, two things happen: (1) they reinforce the capabilities of their traditionally successful mediators by bringing their

[77] Köngäs Maranda, "What Does a Myth Tell about Society?", *Radcliffe Institute Seminars*; *Idem* "Two Tales of Orphans", *Radcliffe Institute Seminars*; *Idem*, Myth and Art as Teaching Materials" *(Educational Services Inc. Occasional Paper 5)*, (Cambridge, Mass.).

exceptional powers together in one individual; but (2) even these reinforced mediators fail to improve the natives' lot.[78] Similar structural alterations are also taking place in Javanese folkdrama but there increasing social mobility opens up new and rewarding possibilities for traditional mediators.[79]

9.6 *Differences in the outcome*

Our models are based on the difference between beginning and outcome and on (1) the presence or absence of an attempt to bring about this difference when it exists, and (2) the failing, cyclical, or helicoidal result of the attempt. Our models can, of course, be embedded. Long myths usually consist of episodes each corresponding to a model, as in the following hypothetical example where the numbers are those identifying our models and the superscripts give their orientation with respect to the main character.

II^{-} III^{-} III^{+} III^{-} I^{-} IV^{+}

The concatenation of models is illustrated graphically in the next section.

9.7 *Morphology of models*

The following graphs were used in this essay. We now give them in mirror pictures, with the summary formulas introduced in 4.4.

Zero mediation :
Model I $A : \bar{A}$

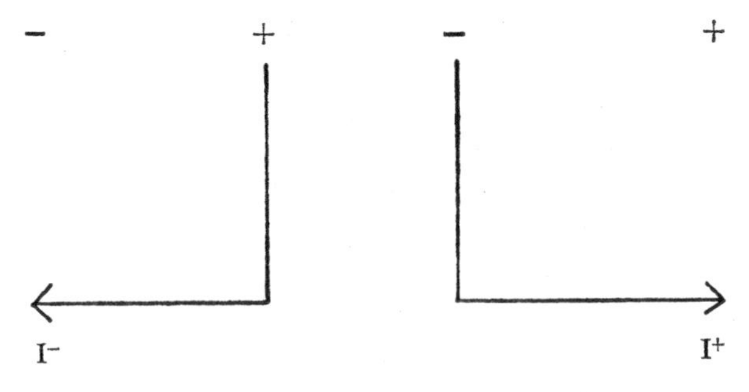

[78] Pierre Maranda, "The Structural Analysis of Myth", Lecture given at Harvard University; cf. Roberto da Matta, "Myth and Anti-Myth among the Timbira", in P. Maranda and E. Köngäs Maranda (eds.), *Structural Analysis of Oral Tradition.*
[79] James Peacock, "Class, Clown, and Cosmology in Javanese Drama : An Analysis of Symbolic and Social Action", in P. Maranda and E. Köngäs Maranda (eds.), *Structural Analysis of Oral Tradition.*

Failing mediation:
Model II $A > B \rightarrow A$

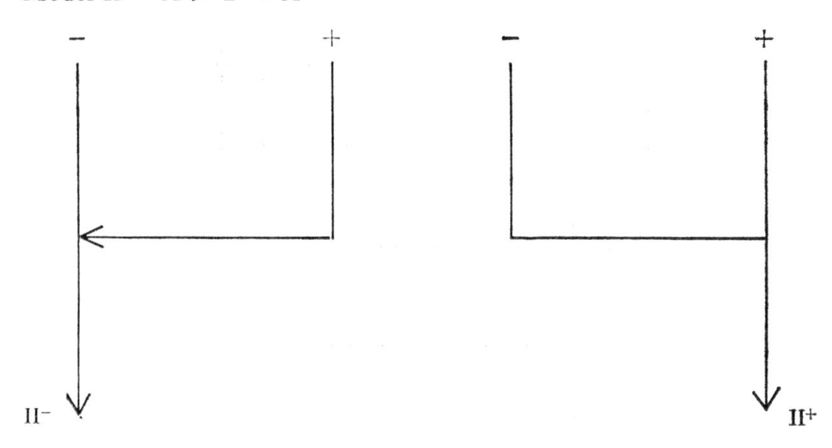

Successful mediation, nullification of the initial impact:
Model III $A < B \rightarrow \bar{A}$

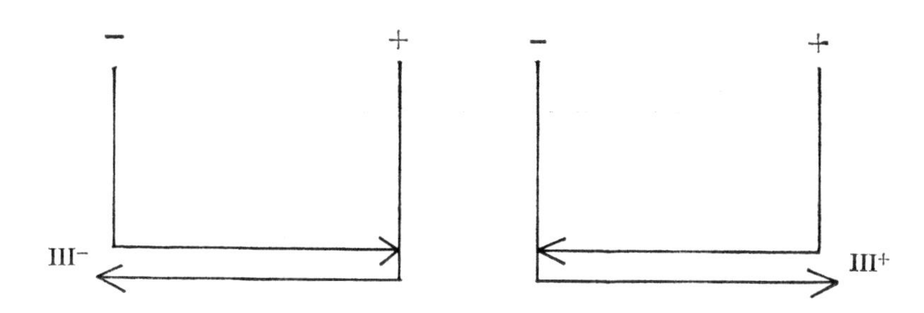

Successful mediation, permutation of the initial impact:
Model IV $A \ll B \rightarrow B$

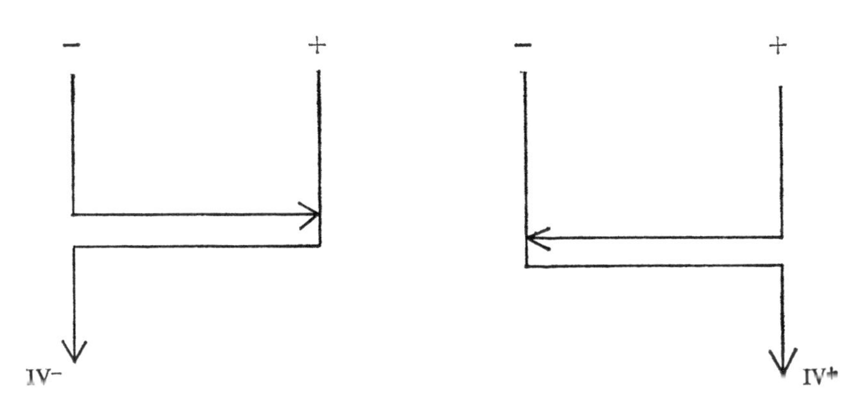

The following figure groups the four models to illustrate their embeddedness.

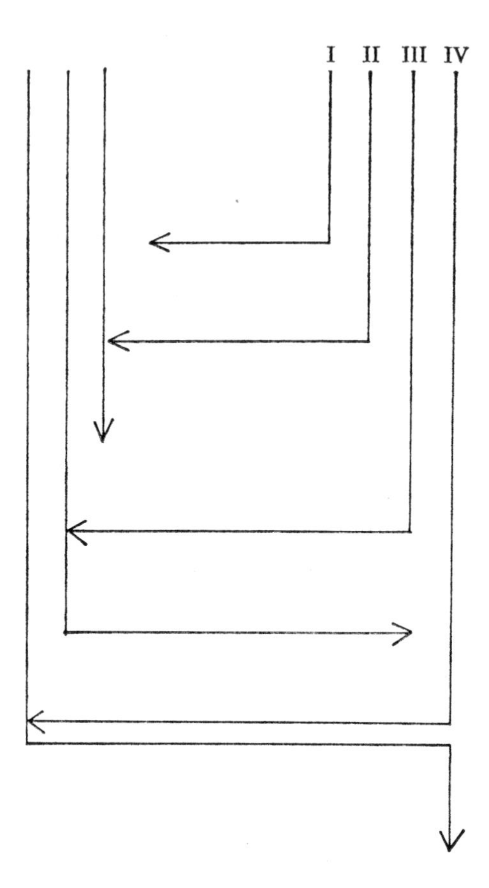

The concatenation at the end of the previous section would be represented thus :

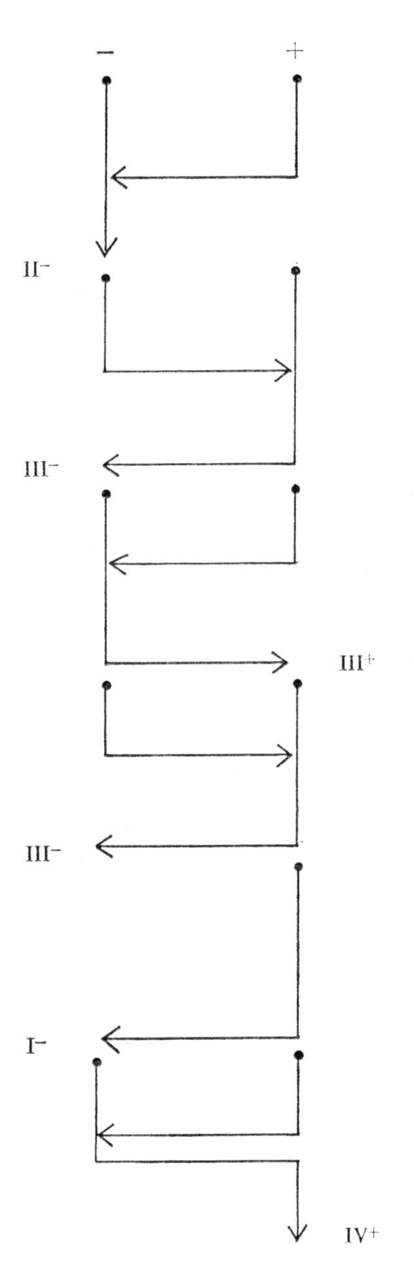

The diagrams can also be drawn as follows; the narrative sequence now advancing from left to right, and the oppositions along the vertical axis :

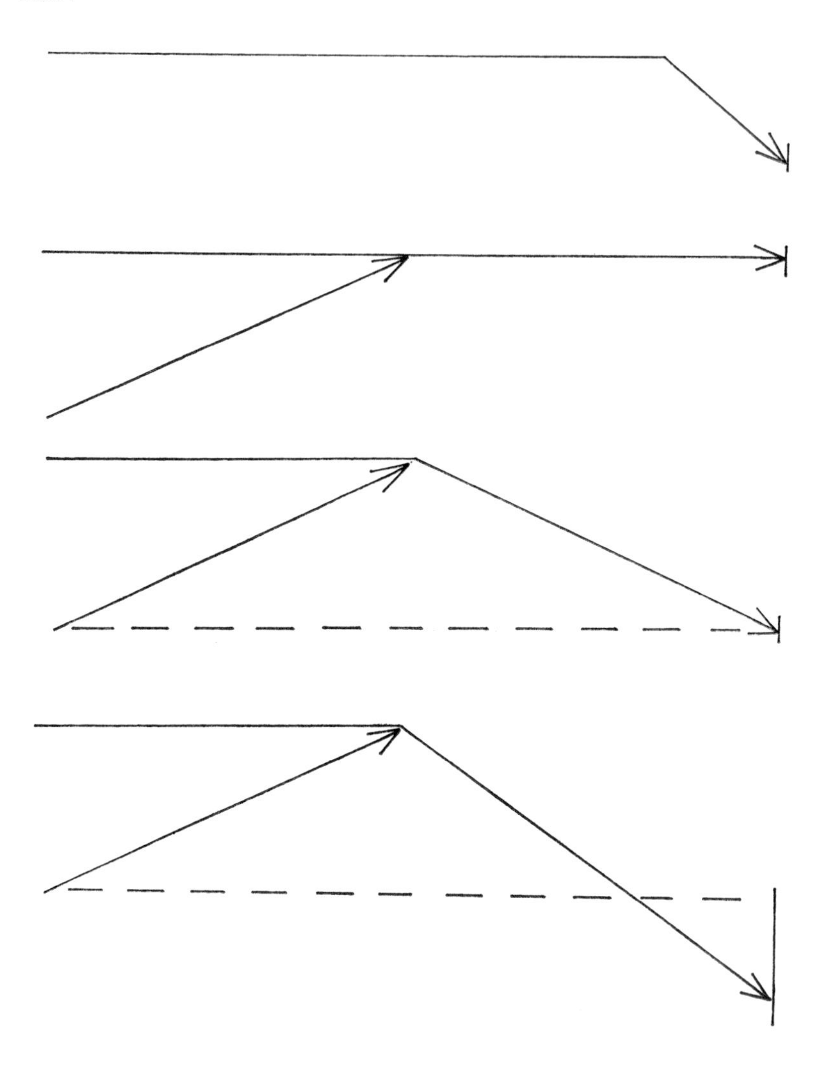

9.8 *Lyric, narrative, and ritual*

On the basis of structural investigation, it seems justified to suggest the following generic distinctions :

Genres	lyric	narrative	ritual
initial contrast	not solved	solved in the narrative itself	solved by the en- and de-coders' participation
plot	non-existent	existent	
mediation	not sought	found in the plot	found outside the plot in the external action
level	subjective	objective	objective to subjective

9.9 *Taxonomic limitations*

Otherwise, it seems that structural study can offer little help for solving problems of folkloristic classification. This is, after all, intelligible: such (as themselves meaningful and practical) distinctions as that between *märchen* and *sage* are based on the function (*märchen* being used for entertainment *sage* for reinforcement of beliefs), but we distinguish between functional and structural aspects.

9.10 *Structure and psychosocial function*

It is an entirely different thing that a structural study can show the slots for, *e.g.*, functions and generic division on that basis. In our formulas, the function has its slot in the last member of the formula. If this slot be filled with a cosmogonic message, we would have a myth; if with a social, we would have, for example, a tale of protest; if with an intellectual message, we might find our item to be a riddle, and so forth. We do not want to draw any definite conclusions as to details at this point, since we have not investigated a wide enough stock of materials.

9.11 *The use of Lévi-Strauss' formula*

Our starting point was to test Lévi-Strauss' formula. We found that it suits the structure of myths but had to develop three other formulas before all our materials could be described. Lévi-Strauss' formula was established to describe the structure of myths.[80] We found it, in a way different from his use, applicable to some other genres as well.[81]

[80] For a use of the formula to investigate the elementary structure of kinship, see P. Maranda, "Note sur l'élément de parenté", *Anthropos* 58 (1963), 810-828.

[81] If the generalizations by Joseph Campbell about hero myths can be accepted (*The Hero with a Thousand Faces* [New York, 1960]), myths of different cultures would indeed fit our formula. Campbell (p. 30) sums up hero myths : "A hero ventures from the world of common day into a region of supernatural wonder : fabulous forces are there encountered and a decisive victory is won : the hero comes back from this mysterious adventure with the power to bestow boons on his fellow men." He illustrates this generalization with examples of Prometheus, Jason, Aeneas, and Buddha; and he diagrams it as a circle representing the hero's movement away from and back to the "world of common day". We want to emphasize — see our model IV — that the hero does not just return to his point of departure as implied by the circle diagram — see our model III — but that the consequence of his adventure is a transformation of the world.

III. OF BEARS AND SPOUSES TRANSFORMATIONAL ANALYSIS OF A MYTH[1]

PIERRE MARANDA

1. OPERATIONAL CONCEPTS

In mathematics, conventional signs between numbers show how these are related, and they enable one to perform operations like additions, subtractions, multiplications, divisions, comparisons, etc. Thus, $3 + 3$ means that a relation of addition is established between 3 and 3 : and $3 + 3 = 6$ states that the two 3's in such a relation of addition are in a further relation of equality with 6; more generally, this means that "IF a given type of relation exists, THEN a specific consequence follows". The proposition "if... then..." is an important logical fact where a necessary connection is expressed; it is commonly represented by an arrow (→) pointing from the antecedent (if...) to the consequent (then...) and it can be read as "yields", so that we can write equivalently $3 + 3 = 6$ or $3 + 3 \rightarrow 6$.

Some such conventional signs will be used in the following analysis. The advantage will be the same as in mathematics, that is, the signs will serve to express clearly and concisely types of relations between the components of myths. They will also make possible analytic and synthetic operations. Ten signs will be used : $+$, $-$, $=$ or $\equiv$, $>$ and $<$, .../...≡.../..., →, comma, and parentheses. The first sign, $+$, will have its current additive meaning and stand for "plus" or "with", *i.e.*, for an "inclusion"; the second, $-$, will have its current subtractive meaning and stand for "minus" or "without", i.e., for "exclusion"; $>$ and $<$ will also be used in their current comparative meaning and stand respectively for "greater than" or "more than" and "smaller than" or "less than"; $=$ and $\equiv$ will be used in the sense of "equal to" and "equivalent to", respectively; .../... ≡ .../... is the usual expression of proportion, i.e., "this is to that (this/that) as this other thing is to

[1] This paper is a version revised in 1965 of a paper written for the unit "Man, A Course of Study", (Cambridge, Mass., Educational Services).

that other one"; $\rightarrow$ will have its usual logical meaning of "yields" or "entails"; the comma between two or more elements will mark pairing or grouping; finally, parentheses will be used whenever elements are together as a whole within a larger context. This operational language will become clearer during the analysis but before beginning the investigation of the texts, "equivalence" and "analogy" must be defined in greater detail.

1.1 *Equivalence*

As a rule symbolized by $=$, or, more adequately, by $\equiv$ or $\simeq$, "equivalence" means that a given thing in a given context fulfills the same role, or can be defined in the same way, as another one in another context. Thus, for mathematicians (who call it equality), $4 + 4 = 8$, and $(3 + 1) + (2 + 2) = (4 + (5 - 1))$ means that it is the same thing to have either side of the equation. For naturalists, the fin of a fish is equivalent to the wing of a bird, and, with respect to them, water is equivalent to air. So, we can write in a convenient form :

$$\text{FIN} \equiv \text{WING}$$
$$\text{WATER} \equiv \text{AIR}$$

or, more adequately,

$$(\text{FIN, WATER}) \equiv (\text{WING, AIR})$$

But this equivalence holds because of the fish on the one hand and the bird on the other. In order to examine more closely the nature of the connection between (FIN, WATER) and (WING, AIR), we will resort to the concept of analogy.

1.2 *Analogy*

Called "proportion" in mathematics, this concept was formed by Aristotle as an instrument to scrutinize the structure of an object of knowledge, and it is still one of the basic tools of modern science. 'Analogy' means essentially that two things can be compared because they have something in common. Thus $1/2 = 2/4$ means that the relation between 1 and 2 on the one hand and 2 and 4 on the other is the same, viz., that of one half, and it reads "1 is to 2 as 2 is to 4", and $3/6 = 4/8$ means the same thing as the previous equation.

But there is a difference between these two examples since in the first one a thing, 1, is to another thing, 2, as this SAME other thing, 2, is to a THIRD thing, 4, whereas in the second example a thing, 3, is to another thing, 6, as a THIRD thing, 4, is to a FOURTH one, 8 : in the first example we have three elements, and four in the second. To be adequate, the definition of analogy must therefore take into account those types. Aristotle proposed to call the first one "continuous analogy" and the second "discontinuous analogy", and the names are well given since, in a comparison between three things measured two by two against each other ($1/2 = 2/4$; $A/B \equiv B/C$) there is a "continuation" of the first pair of things into the other, *i.e.*, a redundant element which links the two poles of the comparison (2, or B, in the example just given).

Discontinuous analogy, which is somewhat more abstract for it does not include a repeated element and therefore focuses on the relations themselves between each pair of elements, is the one where a rapport between two things on the one hand is compared to another rapport between two OTHER things on the other hand; thus, $3/6 = 4/8$, and $A/B \equiv C/D$ are examples of discontinuous analogy.

In the numerical examples given above, the sign expressing the equivalence is the common equality sign, $=$, but in the examples consisting of letters, we see that it is $\equiv$: this is because in numerical propositions implying whole numbers or exact fractions which have not been rounded up, the relation is that of exact equality whereas, when the things set in the proportion are not exactly equal in the mathematical sense, the equivalence sign is preferred.

The case of equivalence quoted in the preceding section can now be processed as an analogy :

WATER/FISH ≡ AIR/BIRD
FIN/FISH ≡ WING/BIRD
WATER/(FIN, FISH) ≡ AIR/(WING, BIRD)

This discontinuous analogy is more revealing than the mere equivalence between terms which was pointed out earlier for it makes clear how FIN ≡ WING, viz., by reference to the things they belong to as fulfilling a locomotor function.

The concepts to be used, and the signs to represent them, are thus :

inclusion : $+$
exclusion : $-$
comparison, greater than : $>$
comparison, less than : $<$

equivalence : $\equiv$
analogy : $.../... \equiv .../...$
consequence : $\rightarrow$
clusters of elements : [...(...)...]

These signs all stand for syntagmatic connections between paradigmatic sets. The latter will be designated by abbreviations (H for husband, W for wife, S for seal, s for snow, etc.).

2. OF BEARS AND SPOUSES: NETSERSUITSUARSSUK AND SIGFITUSUARSSUK THE LAME

The two myths which will be analyzed briefly, and the third one which will be added as a supplement in part 3 *(The Woman Who Heard Bears Speak)* are concerned with bears and married couples, and they throw light on the couple as a unit in Eskimo life, hunting practices, bears, the contrast between wilderness and home, and the conception of magic and the supernatural. The two first myths will be taken up one after the other; a comparative analysis will follow, the result of which will be verified against the information supplied in the third myth. For the sake of convenience, I call these three myths M_1, M_2, and M_3.

2.1 M_1, *Netsersuitsuarssuk*

Netsersuitsuarssuk was the name of a man who never could catch seals. When his neighbors came home with their catch, he never had anything. At last his wife became angry with him and refused to give him any water to drink when he came home from hunting at the breathing holes. In that way he lived for some time out with the other men during the day at the breathing holes, but when he came home his wife would give him no water to drink.

At last he started wandering, and he walked on and on and did not come home when it was night. He came to a big house where three bears lived. For a time he stayed with them, and then returned to his village.

When he got home, he asked his wife as usual for water to drink but she would give him none. Then Netsersuitsuarssuk turned around and gazed stiffly and incessantly at the side platform and at once the snow outside began to creak with the footfalls of a bear. It was his new helping spirit and the window of the house was smashed in with a blow of a bear paw. "Here is some water!" cried his wife and at once the bear left the house without doing them any harm. After that Netsersuitsuarssuk got all the water he wanted to drink when he came home from hunting, and now the strange thing happened that, although he had never been able to catch a seal, after the bear's visit to his house he became a great seal hunter who killed many seals. (Told by Samik; K.Rasmussen, 1931 : 416-417).

The beginning of the myth implies that the normal situation in a house is that the husband supplies the food and the wife provides the drink (seal and water, respectively); this can be diagrammed as in fig. 1.

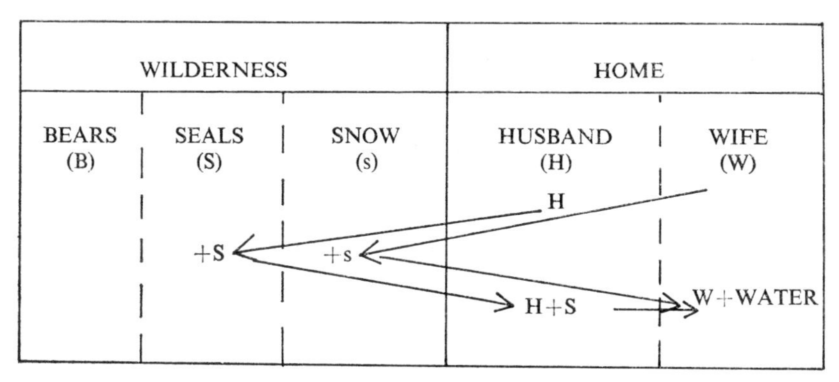

Fig. 1 : The Normal Situation in an Eskimo Home as Implied in M_1 : Husband as Purveyor of Game, Wife as Supplying Water upon his Return.

But in the myth, the husband is incapable of fulfilling his role, so his wife refuses to perform hers; see fig. 2.

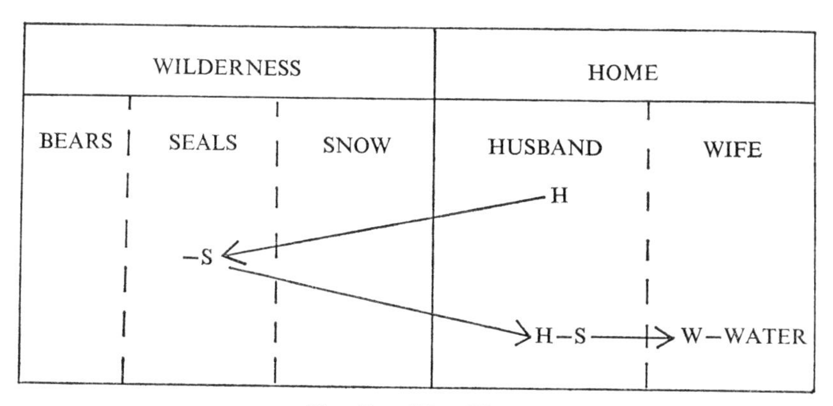

H — S → W — Water

Fig. 2 . The Situation in the Eskimo Home Depicted in M_1.

The difference between fig. 1 and fig. 2 lies in the change of sign before S (for seal) : the "addition" to the household of the seals caught by the husband entails a supply of water by the wife; the "subtraction", or lack, of seal entails that of water. The same fact can be expressed in the two contrasting formulas at the bottom of each figure ($H + S \rightarrow W + \text{Water}$, and $H - S \rightarrow W - \text{Water}$).

Then H leaves his house and wanders in the wilderness where he meets bears and spends some time with them (fig. 3).

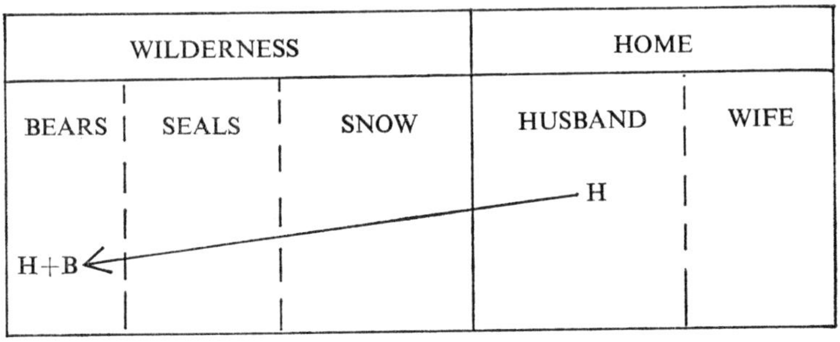

WILDERNESS | HOME
BEARS | SEALS | SNOW | HUSBAND | WIFE
H
H+B

Fig. 3 : Netsersuitsuarssuk with the Bears.

When the husband returns home, his wife gives him water out of fear, for a bear smashes the window of the house with his paw; thus, H, without an S but with a B gets water (fig. 4).

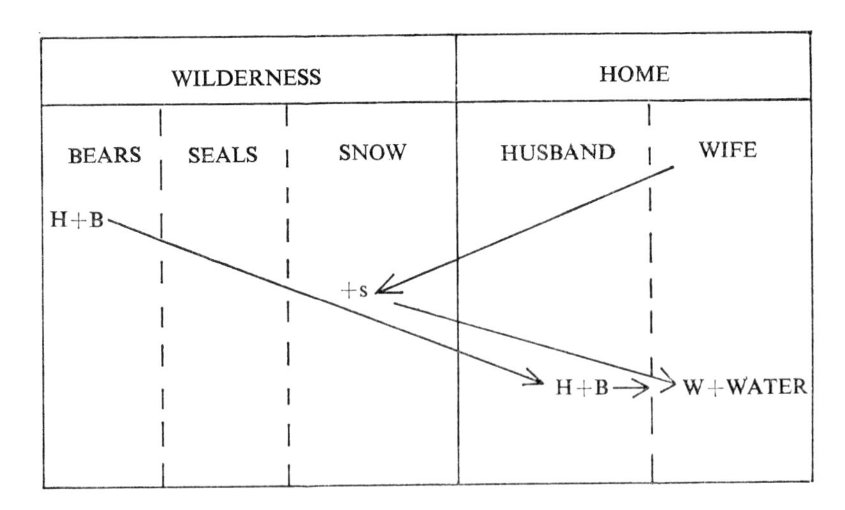

Fig. 4 : $(H-S+B) \rightarrow (W+\text{WATER})$

And then, the man succeeds in killing seals so that the situation becomes normal in his house (see fig. 1).

The whole story can now be restated (1) with the help of a diagram and (2) with the help of formulas which summarize the plot.

(1) Diagram of M_1; see fig. 5.

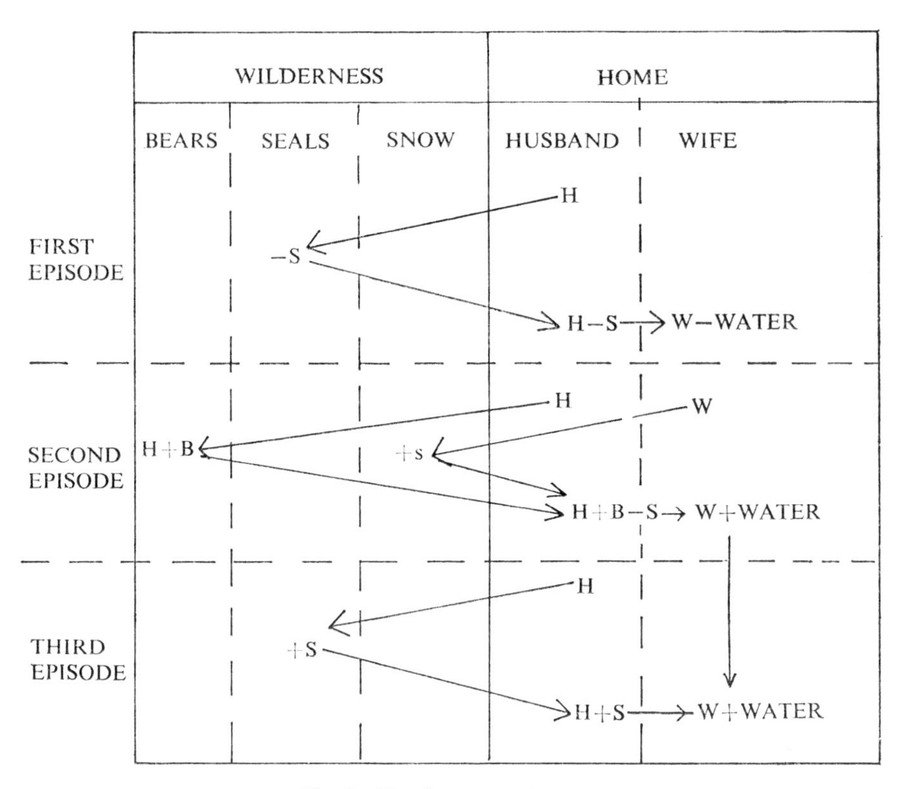

Fig. 5 : The Structure of M_1.

(2) Formalization of M_1 :

First episode : (H — S) → (W — Water)
Second episode : (H — S + B) → (W + Water)
Third episode : (H + S) → (W + Water)

The myth is clear enough on the whole : let the man contribute his share to the life of his household, and his wife will cooperate; otherwise, he will have to have her threatened to get what he needs. But two important questions remain to be answered for the interpretation to be satisfactory. (1) How is it that the presence of the bear makes the wife give water to her husband? Does she do it out of fear of the bear? (2) How does the husband become a successful hunter after his stay with the bears and the visit of his helping spirit?

The second question will be taken up first for its answer will throw light on the first one. In the Arctic, polar bears live on seals, among other preys, and they are powerful hunters. Thus, the stay of the husband with the bears imparts him the power of a good hunter, of a good seal catcher: he now participates in the might of bears, he has a bear as helper, he has the 'soul' of a bear.

Now, to answer the first question, it could be said that the wife is afraid not so much of the bear himself (whom she does not see but only hears) as of her husband who now has the soul and power of a bear; in fact, it is evident that it is for fear of him, after his gazing "stiffly and incessantly at the side platform" which the wife interprets as the calling of the bear, that she gives him water.

The message of the myth is thus that a situation of disequilibrium caused by exclusion can be corrected and equilibrium reestablished by inclusion. The inversion of signs (two minus in the initial situation to two plus in the outcome), *i.e.*, the reestablishment of equilibrium, is due to the new power acquired by the husband: that of frightening his wife and that of catching seals. The myth narrates how the husband conquers his domestic and economic roles thanks to the intervention of the bear. The latter therefore behaves as a mediator which fulfills the function of magical helper. A fairly constant strategy — exemplified in a great many initiation rites — for an individual in need is to leave the ordered, known domestic domain and to wander in the wilderness where cosmic and chaotic forces operate freely. There the individual risks to perish; but he may also encounter a powerful helper who will bestow new capabilities on him. Thus, the individual will receive a new strength which will enable him to participate better in the life of his society. In this case as in many others, he will from then on command respect in his household by inspiring fear if needed, and he will do as well as his fellow men by their common standards.

2.2 *M_2, Sigfitusuarssuk, Who killed a Bear with his Stick*

It is told that a lame man was out looking for a blubber cache with his wife. They came across bear tracks and began to follow them.

The lame man had no other weapon than his stick. His wife he left behind, having told her to build a snow hut where they could sleep.

The lame man got up to the bear, which was lying asleep. Then he said magic words that were to make it sleep soundly. When it was in a deep sleep he lifted its strong little tail with his stick and then drove it into its rump. The bear rose up, but fell back on its end and the stick, which struck against the ice, went right up its backside and killed it.

In that way, the lame man killed a bear and, when he got home, he said to his wife : "I have got a skin for you to chew on the fat off." At first she would not believe him, for of course he had gone out without weapons.

These are the magic words the lame man used for soothing the bear to sleep :

"You with the many glands, you with the many glands
Fall sound asleep, fall sound asleep.
You, who are hard to kill,
You, strong of gland, hang your strong glands
Up beside you,
You, who are hard to kill, you, strong of glands,
Sju-Sju-Sju." (Told by Nakasuk; K. Rasmussen, 1931 : 292-293).

The myth can be diagrammed as a whole since it should not be necessary to repeat here the steps taken for M_1 :

(1) Diagram of M_2 (fig. 6).

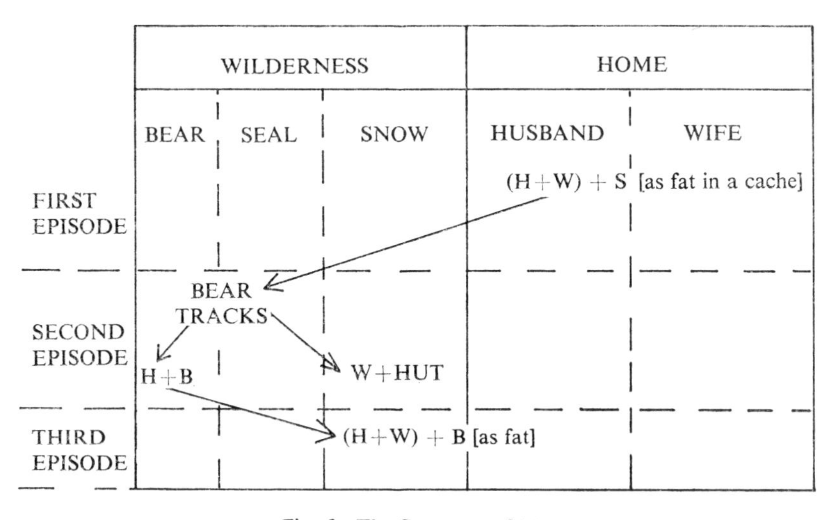

Fig. 6 : The Structure of M_2.

(2) Formalization of M_2:
First episode : (H + W) → BLUBBER CACHE [FAT]
Second episode : (H + B) → (W + HUT)
Third episode : (H + W) → B [FAT]

In this myth, we are in presence of a married couple, as in M_1, but this time the husband is not trying to kill seals: on the contrary, the couple already has blubber stored in a cache and both the husband and his wife are on their way to get it. Then, the encounter of the husband and the bear has a completely different outcome than in M_1. In order to understand M_2 better, which should also help with M_1, let us compare the two narratives.

2.3 *Comparison of M_1 and M_2*

As far as the personages are concerned, the same types are staged: a husband and his wife, seals, bears; and the setting is the same, too, that is, in both cases, the wife belongs chiefly to the home while the husband goes after a prey. But, in M_2, as said above, the seals do not have to be caught since their blubber is already stored in a cache; moreover, while a bear figures as hunting helper in M_1, it becomes hunted, and prey, in M_2; then, in M_2, the wife in no way shows hostility or

TABLE 1

Comparison of M_1 and M_2

M_1	M_2
H and W lack fat; H could never catch a seal, and his W becomes angry and refuses to give him a drink.	H and W have more fat than they consume, they have blubber stored in a cache and go together for it.
H wanders in the wilderness and comes to a bears' house where he stays for some time.	In the wilderness, they come across bears' tracks; H follows them to the bear while W builds a hut.
H returns to his home where his helping spirit frightens his W, who gives water to her H.	H puts the bear to sleep magically and kills it with a stick.
H becomes a successful hunter, and is supplied with water by his W whom he supplies with seal.	H returns to his W with the fat skin of the bear.

exerts sanction against her husband (her only reaction is that of astonishment), contrary to her attitude in M_1. Therefore, M_1 and M_2 are two documents which partly overlap and partly diverge, and the similarities and differences should be instructive. Table 1 summarizes the comparison of M_1 and M_2.

The same comparison can be made more eloquent, and reveal more of the similarities and differences between the texts if we use our formalizations (see fig. 5 for M_1 and fig. 6 for M_2).

	M_1	M_2
FIRST EPISODE	$(H_1 - S_1) \rightarrow (W_1 - \text{WATER})$	$(H_2 + W_2) \rightarrow S_2[\text{FAT}]$
SECOND EPISODE	$(H_1 - S_1 + B_1) \rightarrow (W_1 + \text{WATER})$	$(H_2 + B_2) \rightarrow (W_2 + \text{HUT})$
THIRD EPISODE	$(H_1 + S_1) \rightarrow (W_1 + \text{WATER})$	$(H_2 + W_2) \rightarrow B_2[\text{FAT}]$

Fig. 7: Comparison of the Formalizations of M_1 and M_2.
The elements which are common to both myths have been assigned a subscript to indicate to which myth they belong.

We see in figure 7 that, for M_2, $B \equiv S$ since it is substituted for it as a basic resource of fat; this is confirmed by the relation of equivalence — the analogy — between M_1 and M_2 since:

$$B_1/H_1 \equiv \text{MAGIC}/H_2$$ [B is the source of power of H_1 as MAGIC that of H_2]

and

$$B_2/H_2 \equiv S_2/H_2 \equiv S_1/H_1$$ [(B, s) are prey to H_2 as S to $(H_1 + B_1)$]

Therefore,

$B_1 \equiv$ MAGIC (as magic helper who helps to get prey)
$B_2 \equiv S_{1,2}$ (as prey, basic resource)
$H_1 < H_2$ (H_1 as failing hunter, $< B$; H_2 through unfit for hunting since he is lame and weaponless $> B$).

Which can be tabulated as in Table 2.

TABLE 2

Definition of the main components of M_1 and M_2

	M_1	M_2
HUSBAND	fit to hunt and armed, without knowledge of magic	unfit to hunt and weaponless, with knowledge of magic
BEAR	helper in hunting	prey
SEAL	prey	catch already secured

The shift of prey or, to be more exact, the shift of the bear from hunter in M_1 to prey in M_2 reveals the main shaft of the myth. To take it from the standpoint of the husbands: H_2 and his magic (he knows songs) is more powerful than a bear and, therefore, than H_1 who receives his strength from the bears (he knows bears). In effect, H_2 has already blubber stored, so he does not need to go after seals; and, to this, he adds the catch of a bear, so "hard to kill" in the words of M_2, which he overcomes by his magic and skill, lame and weaponless as he is (while H_1 is not said to be handicapped in any way). Thus M_1 and M_2 taken jointly show that a man without magic and special skill but with a good hunting power has to satisfy himself with seals, but that the one who has magic and skill can also hunt bears successfully even if he is lame and lacks hunting gear. And, if a bear is superior to a common man (as in M_1), it is degraded to an inferior position, that of prey, when facing a man like H_2. Finally, whereas the action of M_1 takes place both in the village and in the wilderness, that of M_2 is entirely located outside the borders of the village. The overlapping messages of the two myths can be represented as in fig. 7a.

$$\overbrace{\underbrace{H_2 > B > H_1 > S}_{M_2}}^{M_1 \,(B > H_1 > S)}$$

Fig. 7a: The Overlapping Messages of M_1 and M_2: the Husband of M_2 is more powerful than the Bear and, therefore, than the Husband of M_1 to whom the bear is superior since it transforms him into a good seal hunter.

And fig. 7a can be made more adequate; see fig. 7b.

	HUNTER	PREY
M_1	(H − MAGIC + B) - - -	- - - - - - → S
M_2	(H + MAGIC) - - - - -	- - - - - - → S + B

Fig. 7b : The Change taking place from M_1 to M_2.

2.4 *A Transformation to Pass from M_1 to M_2 and vice versa*

Figure 7 shows that everything in M_2 bears the sign + which is not the case in M_1 : in other words, the second myth unfolds as an "addition", that is, as a series of inclusions which enrich H_2 whereas the first one starts with a "subtraction", or an exclusion which is cancelled out in the outcome; thus, in M_2, we are told the story of the increase of H_2's success whereas M_1 narrates the less glamorous story of the improvement of H_1's fate. Fig. 7c repeats fig. 7b partly but is more explicit about the relations between H and B.

	HUNTER	PREY
M_1	(H − MAGIC) $<$ B ————	———→ S
M_2	(H + MAGIC) $>$ B ————	———→ S + B

Fig. 7c : Dominance Relations between H and B.

It is now very simple to pass from one myth to the other : let us change the sign before MAGIC in fig. 7c. In effect the inversion of the first sign in M_1 (the − denoting the lack of magic becoming a + to denote its presence) yields M_2 since then $H_1 < B$ becomes $H_2 > B$, and B passes accordingly from the side of the hunter to that of prey; a similar inversion of the sign in M_2 yields M_1. And the two myths can now be expressed in a single formula :

$$(H \pm \text{MAGIC}) \gtrless B \rightarrow S \pm B$$

The paradigms remain the same, which implies that both myths explore the same semantic universe. The difference is of a syntagmatic order : the exploration shows the superiority of the knowledge of magic over the common physical strength of a hunter possessing only a spirit helper. The two different syntagmatic chains relate the paradigms in a fashion congruent with the 'prestressed' character of the two heroes. In effect, *Netsersuitsuarssuk* consists of /*nettiq*/, 'seal', /*suit*/, 'never', /*suar*/, 'big', and /*ssuk*/, 3rd pers. sing., whereas *Sigfitusuarssuk* means 'he who is a big lame'.[2] The myths show how the one who was a failing hunter became a successful one (Model III) and how a lame and weaponless man who knows magic is not only better off at the outset (he already has blubber stored to begin with) but will even achieve exceptional feats (Model IV).

2.5 *Residues*

So far, the analysis has focused on the core of the myths; it is now time to reintegrate the domestic prestations left aside above (cf. figure 7), viz., that of water for seal and that of the building of the snow hut. A comparison of the relations present in M_1 and M_2 (see fig. 5 and 6) shows that we have in M_1 a consequence which does not figure in M_2, the negative "$- \rightarrow -$", *i.e.,* "if no seal, then no water". Actually, it is clear enough that this negative feature, or "subtraction", has no room in the "additive" M_2. The sanction exerted by W_1 against her husband springs from the failure of the latter, which is without parallel in M_2. In point of fact, W_1 and W_2 are in contrast with respect to their attitudes toward their husbands. Both are mentioned in connection with normal domestic duties (melting snow, and hut building, tedious jobs devolved upon women in Eskimo society); the refusal of W_1 and the readiness of W_2 to fulfill their respective roles are consistent in their respective contexts as well as with respect to each other in the ensemble formed by M_1 and M_2. A last comprehensive formula can summarize the two myths without important residues; see fig. 8.

$$\frac{(H_2 + \text{MAGIC}) > \overline{B > [(H_1, S) + (W_1, \text{SNOW})]}^{\,M_1} \rightarrow S + B}{M_2}$$

Fig. 8 : Comprehensive Formalization of M_1 and M_2.

[2] I am indebted to Dr. Jean Briggs for this explanation.

3. TEST OF THE APPROACH

The structure of this paper conforms to that of its composition : M_1 was encountered, read, and analyzed first; then M_2 was included because of its similarities with the first one. But then a third myth turned up, closely related to M_1 and M_2 : it was not analyzed before its 'cognates' were processed. It will now be quoted, and a few remarks will be made since it can confirm, question, or modify the interpretation proposed for M_1 and M_2 — this will provide an opportunity to test the approach presented in part 2.

3.1 *M_3, The Woman Who Heard Bears Speak*

There was once a woman who ran away from home because she was angry with her husband. She had a baby with her in her amaut. She walked and walked and came to a house where there was no one at home. It was just like an ordinary house for people, and so she went in. Everybody was out hunting. They were bears in human form, and they became her helping spirits from the moment she went in to them.

In the evening, when they returned from hunting, she crawled in behind the seal-skin hangings that line the interior of a snow hut. The bears were great hunters, and they had a fine, big snow hut lined throughout with beautiful seal skins. From her hiding place the woman could hear what the bears spoke about while they fed, eating only the fat of their kill as bears do.

There were an old couple and their sons. The youngest of the sons was young, inexperienced and gave himself such airs. He spoke about the breathing hole hunting of humans, saying: "Those shin-bone figures are terribly thin below. One almost feels inclined to knock them down."

His parents, however, remonstrated : "It's not so easy to tackle those shin-bone figures. They have hunting gear and their dogs to help them."

This was how bear speech sounded — no other than the woman could understand it. The old people warned the young one to keep his head, but all to no purpose. The next day he went man-hunting just the same. He was young and disobedient. Evening came and they waited in vain for his return but he did not come. He had tried to attack some humans, and they killed him. Not till the fourth day after did he come home, and then he had a harpoon head hanging in his fur.

He had learned that it was dangerous to attack people, and he now told of everything he had gone through. He had tried to hunt the slender shin-bone figures that walked about upright on two legs, but when they set their dogs on him he had turned frightened and had run away. The dogs, however, were faster and did not get out of breath; they got up to him when he himself had to stop to get his wind and eat snow, and they nipped his tail. As soon as they bit his tail he became so strangely slack at the knees and sat down, feeling no inclination at all to run away. In the meantime the shinbone figures got up to him and, when they simply pointed at him with something that looked like a rod, he suddenly felt a scorching heat in his body; he became so faint that he simply threw himself down on the snow. Then they all surrounded him and he got up with difficulty to run, but again the dogs were there and nipped his tail, so he had to sit down again. Once more the men pointed at him, and inexpressibly tired he fell over and became unconscious.

Thus the bear was killed by the humans, and they gave him a death taboo that was as it should be; for four days his soul rested among many splendid presents in the house of the humans. Then he was free again and could come back home, rich in experience and with great respect for the shin-bone figures whom he had previously despised.

The woman got well away from the house of the bears and told the people of her village what she had gone through. From that experience people have obtained proof of how important it is that a dead bear's soul gets the right taboo. For the strongest thing of all life here is the soul. (Told by Mnelaq, Rasmussen, 1931 : 218-219.)

This third myth about "bears and spouses" presents a number of points of contact with M_1 and M_2, and it provides some interesting supplements of information. The first paragraph shows a wife (W_3) leaving her home, coming to a bears' house and, by that very fact, receiving bears as helping spirits, whereas, in M_1, it was the husband who left his home (because his wife, W_1, was angry at him as W_3 is angry at her own husband), came to the house of the bears who became his helping spirits. Then M_3 supplies detail, absent from M_1, about the house of the bears; it also confirms the interpretation that H_1 becomes a good seal hunter after a bear, a powerful seal hunter, becomes his helping spirit (the presence of beautiful seal-skin hangings); likewise, M_3 refers to the association we found implicit in M_2 between blubber, bear, and fat.

In the bears' house, we meet an old couple and their sons. No such mention of family relations between bears exists in M_1 or M_2 — M_1

speaks only of "three bears" — no more than M_1 tells about the decoration of the house : probably because M_3 is longer than the two others. (This illustrates the difference between content and structure : although additional details, descriptions, digressions, etc., provide often useful grounds for the interpretation of wholes, they do not alter the course of action which only forms the structure of the story.) But here we have a situation converse of that of M_1 and M_2 and of the adventure of W_3, since it is a bear that leaves its home (in the wilderness) to go to the Eskimo people and attack them just as Eskimos leave their houses to attack game and as H_1 and W_3 leave their home to go to the bears'. This inversion parallels the intervention of B_1 coming to H_1's house, but then it is to help, not to attack him.

The young and adventurous bear is killed by the people so that we should write here B_3 < HUNTERS but, to be adequate, we must keep in mind that the bear is YOUNG and that the Eskimos are hunting IN GROUP and with the help of their DOGS so that the relation is

$$\text{YOUNG BEAR} < (\text{HUNTERS} + \text{DOGS})$$

— and it may be worth recalling that Eskimo dogs belong definitely to an intermediary category : carnivorous animals which share in their masters' kill, they are also man's servants, the only domesticated animals. The catch of the bear is told in a way which reminds one of M_2, especially the reference to the tail of the bear as a most vulnerable point.

It would be too long to deal here with M_3 in full : the idea is only to check the validity of the previous interpretations against new data. M_3 implies additional elements which, to be explained, would require that other myths be brought in (like *The Creation of Live Game and All Taboo*, Rasmussen, 1931 : 212-213) as well as ethnographic data (like female shamanism among the Netsilik). Only what of M_3 is isomorphic to M_1 and M_2 will be retained as diagrammed in fig. 9 (where it will be convenient to make a special heading for a category which, in previous diagrams, was not singled out, that of "supernatural" as including both its "aggressive"—magic— and "defensive" — compliance with a prescription — aspects).

In all three myths, bears and spouses interact with each other in a sort of reserved mutual respect; magic or ritual practices intervene when bears are killed, and it is also evident that bears possess a mysterious power which they can communicate.

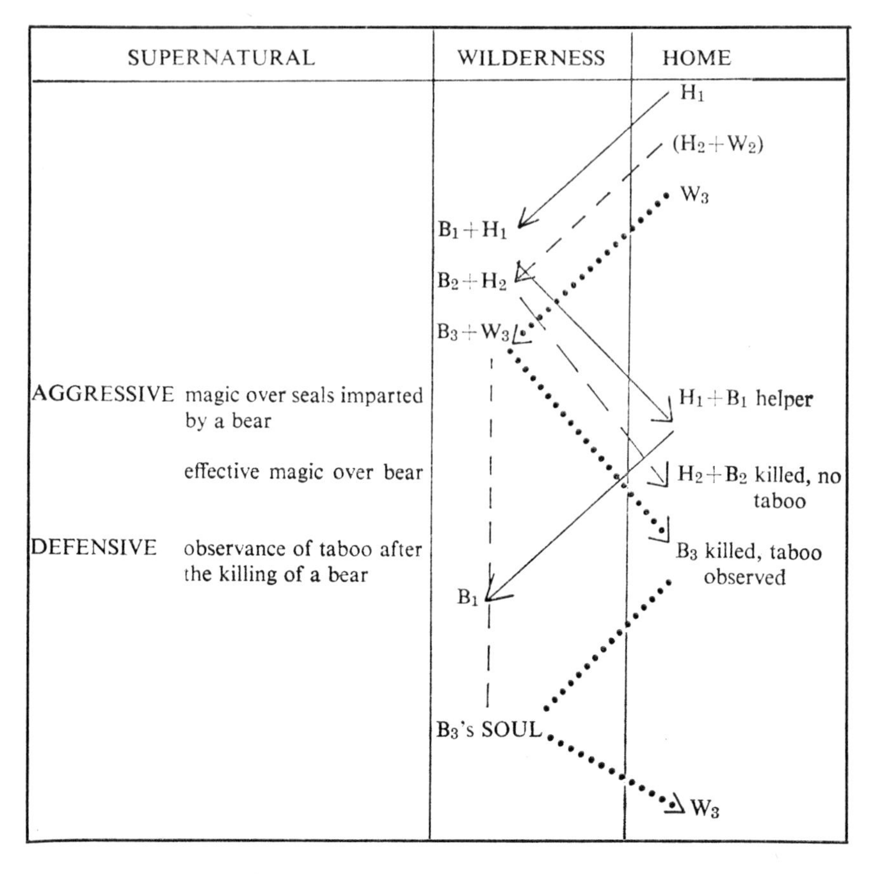

Fig. 9 : The Structure of M_1, M_2, and M_3.

3.2 *Second Transformation Rule to Pass from M_1 and M_2 to M_3*

We already know that we can pass from M_1 to M_2 (see fig. 7c); fig. 10 will help see how M_2 can now be transformed into M_3.

	SUPERNATURAL AGGRESSIVE	AGGRES SOR		AGGRESSION AGAINST		VICTIM	SUPERNATURAL DEFENSIVE
M_2	(MAGIC + MAN)		$\gtrless$	BEAR	$\rightarrow$	BEAR	
M_3		BEAR	$\gtrless$	MAN	$\rightarrow$		(BEAR + TABOO)

Fig. 10 : see text; $\gtrless$ stands for "competition".

To pass from M_2 to M_3, therefore, we have only to make a paradigmatic change, that of agressor from man to bear, which entails a paradigmatic AND syntagmatic transformation, viz., supernatural shifts from initial aggressive to terminal defensive (which is consistent with the nature of magical and ritual practices in general). A complementary transformation is possible from M_1 to M_3 : this time, if B passes from helper (M_1) to aggressor (M_3), then it is killed (M_3) and the supernatural power it gave to man in M_1 is reciprocated, so to speak, in an inverse form, that of the death taboo (passage from aggressive to defensive magic). The three myths can accordingly be considered as transformations of the same core, and as stressing the same message from different angles. The complete series is :

M_1 to M_2 : A bear will be the hunting helper of a man who does not possess magic, and the prey of one who possesses magic. (H_1 can thus become a respected member of society by being feared by his wife and catching seals; on the other hand, given H_2's magic, blubber is already stored, his wife is submissive, and the bear becomes an additional source of fat.)

M_1 to M_3 : If a bear shifts from the helper to the aggressive function, he becomes victim and he is killed without the help of magic but by a GROUP of hunters and their DOGS. Then a ritual must be performed *post factum*. (Bears are supernaturally loaded and automatic dispensers of magic to whomever shares in their lives — M_1; when they enter in hostile contact with humans and perish in the venture, supernatural is paid back to them in the form of ritual prestations — M_3.)

M_2 to M_3 : If a man kills a bear with the help of magic, no ritual prestations are mentioned; if a group of hunters and their dogs kill a bear by non-magical means, ritual prestations become of great importance.

M_3 to M_1 : If men are attacked by a bear instead of being given magic, they will kill him and offer ritual prestations; if a man receives magical help from bears, the former will partake of the latter's power and both will exploit the same resources. The series can thus be generated back and forth.

There is also an interesting association between the core of the myths as it appears in the transformation processes and the type of relations between the spouses at the beginning of each of the three myths, as can be seen in fig. 11.

RELATIONS BETWEEN SPOUSES		RELATIONS BETWEEN MAN AND ANIMALS	OUTCOME
M_1	(H − W)	(H − MAGIC) <	B → S
M_2	(H + W)	(H + MAGIC) >	B → (S + B)
M_3	(W − H)	B < (PEOPLE + DOGS) →	(B + TABOO)

Fig. 11 : Relations between spouses and the structure of $M_1 - M_3$.

If there is a necessary connection between the type of relations between spouses and the pay-off in the outcome, as the greater power of the husband (lame and weaponless otherwise) associated with his wife may lead to think, then another transformation enables to pass from M_1 to M_2 to M_3. In effect, if we change the sign between the spouses of M_1, we have M_2 (see figure 7c), and if we do not change the sign but the order of the spouses (or their sex, if we want to keep the order constant), we then have the initial situation of M_3, *i.e.,* (W − H), and then: (1) B takes the initiative and becomes aggressor first and then prey; (2) (H, MAGIC) is replaced by a group of people and their dogs; and (3) "defensive supernatural" emerges as a category, *i.e.,* the supernatural element shifts to a terminal position. Thus, whenever the sign between H and W is −, B is in the position of antecedent: (B → MAGIC), and (B → TABOO) in M_1 and M_3, respectively, whereas when the sign between H and W is +, B is in the position of consequent: (MAGIC) → B in M_2.

4. SUMMARY AND CONCLUSION

Two myths have been considered whose interpretation was sketched by specifying what kinds of connection exist between their components. "Addition", "subtraction", "comparison", "equivalence", "analogy", and "consequence" were the main analytical tools which turned out to be useful in that they made it possible to handle the syntagmatic connections between paradigms. The third myth, which was brought in to test the method, corroborated it. The signs are simple and can be handled easily and without great technical skill. The problems of analysis have been approached from a purely practical standpoint and theoretical angles have been systematically ignored.

How can the message of the three myths be summarized? Harmonious relations between husband and wife seem to lead to greater pay-offs. But then, such relations depend on the ability of the husband to fulfill his role. This, in turn, cannot be done without resorting to magic, in one way or another. And mutual respect must dominate the relations between man and bear: the former may be in possession of a magic more powerful than that imparted to him by the bears, but, otherwise, he must depend on them; on the other hand, bears cannot prevail against man when the latter plays in coalition with other men and dogs. This is a question of delicate balance. Man cannot deal with nature without due consideration and nature will not be inconsiderate of the capabilities of man in his social dimension.

In point of fact, it may be significant that whereas the actions of M_1 and M_3 unfold against a social background (other hunters in M_1 to whom the failing hero is contrasted, a family of bears and a group of hunters in M_3), that of M_2 takes place without reference to society, that of bears or of men. Everything happens as though the only couple who can be staged alone is that where the man possesses exceptional magical powers.

The transformations which enable to pass from one myth to another reveal socio-cosmological vectors. In other words, they show the intersecting paths along which Netsilik thought explores its models of behavior. One's fate will depend on whether a few key switches are opened or closed, with the consequence that one must keep an eye on them in order to survive.

IV. "A TREE GROWS" TRANSFORMATIONS OF A RIDDLE METAPHOR

ELLI KÖNGÄS MARANDA

1. MATERIALS

This essay deals with the transformations of one Finnish riddle metaphor. The materials are taken from an anthology of 3,500 riddles,[1] a representative selection of the 10,000 riddles in the Folklore Archives of the Finnish Literature Society (Haavio and Hautala, 1946). After completing an extensive study of Finnish riddles (Köngäs Maranda, 1969, 1970a, b)[2], I have spent two years in Melanesia in anthropological fieldwork and collected more than a thousand riddles from the Lau of North Malaita, Solomon Islands. Any in depth study of Lau riddles will take some time, and, as it will involve considerable linguistic analysis both as a preliminary and as a part of the exposition, will require more space than is available here. The present essay is an investigation of the properties of the logical structure of riddles and of the processes of generating such structures. The exercise is of necessity somewhat formal, but was not done without knowledge of those aspects that are the basis of a full analysis : the original language and culture, the collecting techniques and classifications used in the Folklore Archives, etc.

2. RIDDLE METAPHORS

There is reason to emphasize that a riddle consists of two parts : the riddle image and the answer. The riddle image is a question (although not always, and not even often, linguistically speaking in the form of a question), and the image is so built that the answer is (logically) contained in it. I realize that there are riddle images with several answers (as well

1 Haavio and Hautala (eds.), *Suomen kansan arvoituskirja*.
2 Köngäs Maranda, "The Logic of Riddles", "Structure des énigmes", and "Perinteen transformaatiosääntöjen tutkimisesta".

as riddle answers corresponding to several images), but this does not make the answer arbitrary.

Central concepts used here are analogy, metaphor, and metonymy. For analogy, Aristotle's definition seems sufficient: "There is an analogy whenever there are four terms such that the relation between the second and the first is similar to that between the fourth and the third" (1475b). This can be presented as

$$A/B = C/D$$

One could also use a notation current in linguistics and anthropology (Lévi-Strauss, Leach),

$$A : B :: C : D$$

Analogy is an operation of the mind. It rests on the recognition of two kinds of relations between the terms: similarity and contiguity, in other words metaphor and metonymy (Jakobson, 1956: 55-82;[3] Leach, 1964). In the analogy formula above, two members in the same structural position (A and C, or, naturally, B and D) constitute a sign (here a metaphor) in which one of them (A) is the SIGNANS or signifier and the other (C) is the SIGNATUM or 'signified' (cf. Saussure, 1916; Jakobson, 1956; Sturtevant, 1960: 2-3; Greimas, 1966: 10).[4]

Finally, the members on one side of the equation mark are in a metonymic relation to each other (A and B). Thus, in the analogy, we have the interrelation of metaphor and metonymy in the same picture:

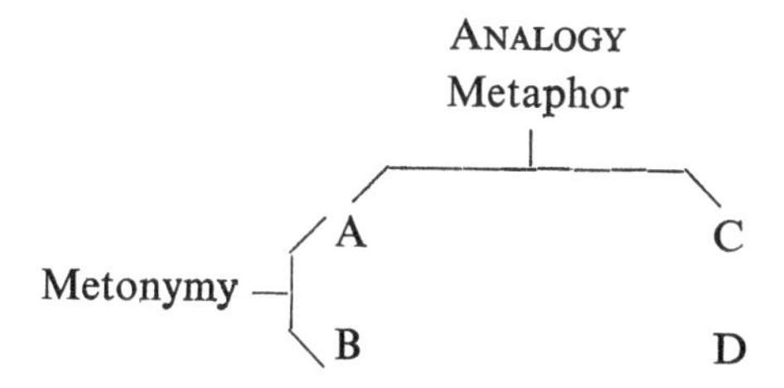

In other words, metonymy is the syntagmatic relation of two terms, metaphor, the paradigmatic equation of two terms.

How are these two terms equated? A metaphor can be considered

[3] Roman Jakobson, "Two Aspects of Language and Two Types of Aphasic Disturbances".

[4] *Cf.* Saussure, *Cours de linguistique générale*; Roman Jakobson and Morris Halle, *Fundamentals of Language*; Edgar H. Sturtevant, *An Introduction to Linguistic Science*, pp. 2-3; A. Julien Greimas, *Sémantique structurale*, p. 10.

a sign consisting of two sets. The identity of the two sets is based on an analogy. If we assign the symbols thus :

A first set,
a one of its elements,
B second set,
b one of its elements,

then we will say that the relations a/A and b/B are each metonymic. The analogy a/A = b/B underlies the equations, that is, the metaphors a = b and A = B. In an everyday metaphor like "the leg of the table", set A would be human beings (or animals), a his (or its) leg, and B table. The metaphor is created by an analogy a/A = x/B, which yields x = leg.

The analogy provides a 'documentation' or at least investigation of the structural identity between the two sets, A and B. In the process, the sets are shown to be subsets (or elements) of a set greater than the two original ones. In the leg metaphor, the superset could be called "standing things". The two original sets, A and B, are superficially opposite, and grounds for the opposition can be named: humans (and animals) are alive, tables are not; humans and animals grow, tables do not; humans and animals have locomotion, tables do not, etc. The metaphor builds a structural bridge over this content abyss.

However, contiguity is the basis of metonymy (cf. Jakobson, 1956).[5] And since riddle metaphors bring the two "opposed" sets into a position where they are shown to be only elements of one superset, then contiguity is established between them, and they are brought into a metonymic relation. This is where metaphors and metonymies, the opposite poles (Jakobson, 1956)[6] of thinking meet. It is unnecessary (but perhaps helpful) to mention that this meeting does not destroy the distinction between metaphors and metonymies, but is only an operation which is an important expression of the rules of analogical thinking. Whether all thinking is finally analogical is not in my interests; this paper is concerned about riddles and the ways in which riddle metaphors are built on analogy.

The signans of a riddle is the core of the riddle image (the term), and the signatum is the answer. The similarity between them is structural, and the riddle image exhibits a documentation of why it is so. But riddle metaphors, at least ideally, differ from the common metaphors of

[5] *Cf.* Jakobson, "Two Aspects of Language...".
[6] Jakobson, "Two Aspects of Language...".

everyday language: the latter are conventional, established, and unambiguous, and for the purposes of language which, after all, is communication, they must so be; in riddle images some hesitation must be created. The meaning of a riddle image must be discovered by following certain rules of the (thinking) game. Like poetic metaphors, riddle metaphors have to offer a fresh insight; but unlike poetry, riddles serve to remind of pre-established orders (that is, if we agree that a poet considers it his task to open new vistas either into linguistic domains or into 'reality').

A peculiarity of riddle metaphors, at least in the corpus which I have studied most, Finnish riddles, is that they are reversible. If A is like B, then B is like A. Not so in everyday language, if we do not think of "wobbly legs" as a countermetaphor of the legs of a table or of a "flood of abuse" as the counterimage of a "mouth of a river".

Riddle structures appear to be of different degrees of complexity: I have distinguished simple, complex, and string riddles (1969 and 1970b).[7] Simple riddles contain only one of each component element; complex riddles have one or more of the elements multiplied, and in string riddles, which I don't include here, the image consists of a list of terms and the answer of another, corresponding list of terms. Certain transformational techniques can be developed to analyze also the different types. I have chosen to name the parts of the riddle structure in the language of logic: the given term (the riddle metaphor), the hidden term (the answer), the true premiss (which holds true of the given term and the hidden term alike and provides a constant), and the false premiss (the pointer, or clue, which shows that the given term is not to be accepted and that the hidden term is to be discovered by way of seeking for an obvious, even if hidden, true premiss to be substituted for the false premiss). The answer of the riddle is to be found in the nullification of the disbalance of the terms and premisses.

3. SIMPLE RIDDLE

I will first take a simple example:

(1) *Mikä juuritta kasvaa*? — *Ihminen.* Haavio-Hautala 4/22 'What [tree] grows without roots? — Human being'.

[7] Köngäs Maranda, "The Logic of Riddles", and "Structure des énigmes".

This riddle is a cross between two truisms :

A tree grows with roots.

A human being grows without roots.

These commonplace truths intersect in the following way :

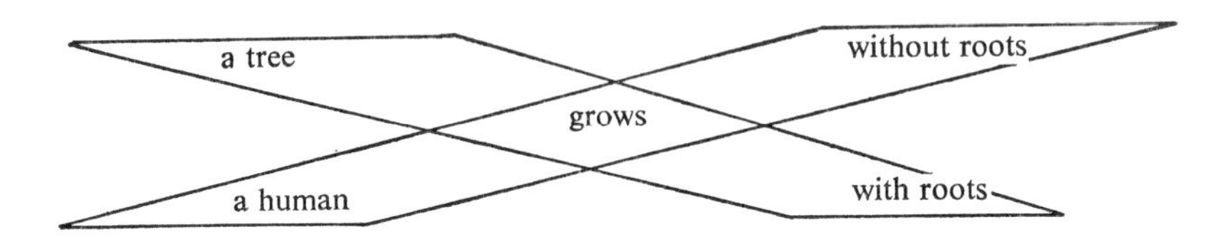

Assigning labels to the different parts of the structure we arrive at the following :

	TERMS	PREMISSES	
		CONSTANT	VARIABLE
GIVEN	a tree (I)	grows (II)	without roots (IV)
HIDDEN	a human being (V)		with roots (III)

The five elements will then be :

I. The given term, which is the signans of the metaphor, the core of the riddle image,

II. the constant premiss, the original point of similarity, which is true both of the signans and the signatum, which is also the transformer,

III. the hidden variable, which is recalled to realize that something is amiss with the statement of the riddle image, that it cannot fit (because trees need roots). By definition, this element is never made explicit, and thus in terms of the utterance itself it always appears as zero,

IV. the given variable, which in turn serves to point at the direction of the answer. This is the condition under which the metaphor holds true,

V. the hidden term, signatum, *i.e.,* the answer.

4. TRANSFORMATIONS

4.1 *Transformations, Series I: Expansion*

Transformations of riddles come about by the expansion of the analogy, that is, by an examination of the correspondence of the two sets in question. The tree metaphor is further specified by adding the analogy

bridal dress/woman = leaves/tree.

The result is the following riddle :

(2) *Pihlaja pyhällä mäellä,*
pyhä lehti pihlajassa. — *Morsian.* 22/1
'A rowan tree on a sacred hill,
sacred leaves in the rowan tree. — Bride [at wedding].'

This time, the constant is implicit. As leaves are only a temporary decoration of a tree, so is the bridal dress only a temporary decoration for the bride.

If the previous transformation considered esthetic aspects, the next turns to 'utility', reproduction :

(3) *Pyhä pihlaja*
pyhän pellon pientarella,
pyhä marja pihlajassa. — *Raskas vaimo.* 23/1
'A sacred rowan tree
on the edge of a sacred field,
a sacred berry in the rowan tree. — Pregnant woman.'

An additional transformation considers the event of birth. In the variants available to me, the riddle posers have made much of the fact that delivery is not a sickness, that birthgiving is a truly creative act. In the following riddle, the tree is said to fall on *raiskio,* which I can translate as ground, but which is more specified than that : it is the ground on which timber is debranched (to be used for construction of houses or just for firewood). On such ground, then, trees which fall meet their rapid death. But, the riddle says :

(4) *Haapa kaatui raiskiolle,*
mutt'ei yhtään oksaa poikki mennyt. — *Synnyttänyt vaimo.* 24/1
'A poplar fell on the ground,
but none of the branches broke. — A woman who has given birth.'

Another riddle carries the same idea :

(5) *Yksi puu kasvaa;*
otetaan viidet saarapuut,
kahdet aatran sarvikot,
ja vielä jääpi puu tuoreeksi. — *Synnyttänyt vaimo.* 25/10

'A tree grows;
five pairs of carrying sticks are taken,
two pairs of plough handles [are taken],
and yet the tree remains fresh. — A woman who has given birth.'[8]

Once born, the child feeds on the mother; but a discrepancy is now felt in the analogy. The sprouting "children" of trees do not need their "mothers". Instead, a forest bird which is often seen pecking on the trunk of a tree is evoked :

(6) *Tikka toukkaa vetää,*
nahkiaista nauvottaa. — *Lapsen imeminen.* 25/3
'A woodpecker pecks for a worm
[parallel line with same meaning]. — The nursing of a child.'

The connection is still metonymic between the woodpecker and the wood; as in English, an allusion is possible in Finnish, where *tikka* 'woodpecker' and *tikku* 'stick' seem at least connected by folk etymology. And as the woodpecker finds its food on the trunk of the tree, pulling the worm out with its beak, so the baby nurses on the mother.

The series of transformations of the tree riddle thus form a description of the life cycle of a woman; and at the end trees fall :

(7) *Kaikki kaatuu, kaikki maatuu,*
[*kaikki mamman poveen mahtuu*]. — *Hauta.* 35/1
'All fall, all turn to earth,
[all find room in mother's chest]. — Grave.'

To maintain that the metaphor — when the image is as abstract as "all" — is between trees and humans, one can recall that "trees die standing", and that, indeed, only humans are buried. I omit here the consideration of the metaphor of earth as mother's body, which as such is interesting and extremely wide-spread (I also collected a corresponding Lau riddle).

[8] The word *saarapuut*, 'forked sticks', is not altogether clear to me; perhaps it, like *sarvikot*, refers to parts of plough, cf. Vilkuna, "Aura, vannas ja ojas", but the uses for the branches are of no importance here.

The whole series of transformations can be mapped thus:

I	II	III	IV	V
Tree	grows	with roots	without roots	human being

transformation 1; transformer "is decorated" →

rowan tree		leaves	bridal dress	bride

transformation 2; transformer "is fertilized" →

rowan tree		berry	embryo	pregnant woman

transformation 3; transformer "reproduces" →

tree (poplar)		branches taken	child born	woman who has given birth

transformation 4, transformer "feeds its dependent" (nurses) →

tree		woodpecker	child	nursing mother

transformation 5, transformer "dies" →

tree		falls	is buried	human being

To clarify my position, I want to mention that Transformation (T) as I use the word in this paper is a PROCESS, transformer (t) an AGENT which operates in this process, and transform designates the end PRODUCT of the process, the riddle variant itself (to which I will now assign the sign R). Whenever I speak of the structure of a riddle, I refer to its constituent structure, and the analysis is of the type of phrase structure analysis; thus, it could be drawn in the form of a tree structure. A series of transformations could then be described thus:

$t_1R \rightarrow R_1$
$t_2R \rightarrow R_2$ or $t_2R_1 \rightarrow R_2$
$t_3R \rightarrow R_3$ or $t_3R_1 \rightarrow R_3$ or $t_3R_2 \rightarrow R_3$

and so forth. An aspect which I have not yet studied in detail is whether transformations necessarily are chains ($R \rightarrow R_1 \rightarrow R_3 \rightarrow \ldots R_n$) or whether several or all transformations can be directly derived from one kernel riddle thus:

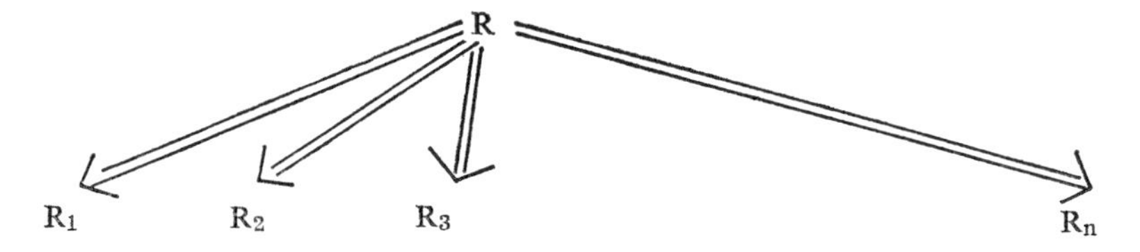

One way of illustrating the process of riddle building would be to consider the "classes" or sets used. At the outset, they are in their proper "order", their customary classificational slots, and do not touch:

The finding of a common function establishes a point of contact, so that the sets become tangential to each other:

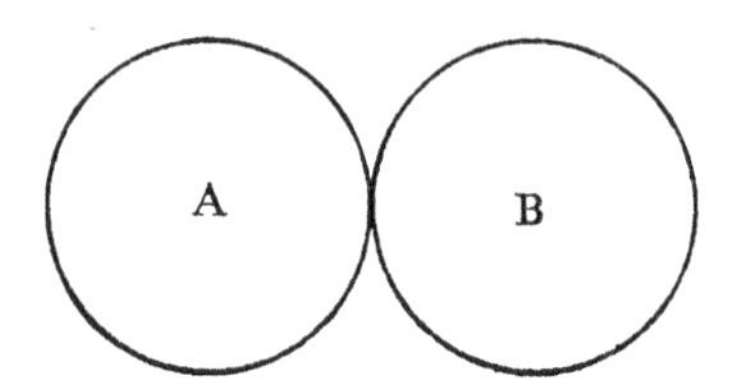

Once the metaphor has been stated, it can be examined by "moves", *i.e.,* transformations which focus on more and more common elements between the two sets:

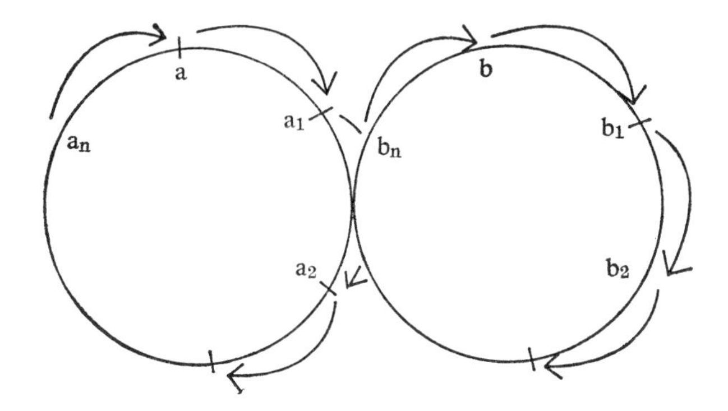

Each element is a "block" or a "stop" or a "station", each transformation is a "move", and each transformer is a "mover". I think at least at this stage that it is important to distinguish between the "stops" and the "movers" : I see the transformers as (logically) verbal statements, and the corresponding pairs of elements as nominal, term-like members of the sets. They are in a metonymic relation to their respective sets and form metaphoric relations in themselves. Thus, riddle transformations appear as analyses of basic metaphors and form wholes in the following way:

$$(A = B) = (a = b) . (a_1 = b_1) . (a_2 = b_2) \ldots (a_n = b_n)$$

Having buried our tree-woman, we can now examine the transforms more closely. We find that the tree is not specified in the two liminal riddles, in the general statement about life, and in the image of death. In a parallel fashion, it is not specified either that the answer is "woman"; it is *ihminen* 'human being'. However, each riddle which specifies the tree, names a leaf tree.

For the time being, it suffices to note that the universe of humans consists of set A = women and its complement $\bar{A}$ = men, and the universe of trees consists of set B = leaf trees and its complement $\bar{B}$ = evergreen trees *(havupuu)*. When projecting the expectation that these would be related in another series of riddles, I do not maintain that all riddle metaphors could possibly have such a neat complement; but here, we can see that by the inversion of the terms complementary riddles could be created.

4.2 *Transformations, Series II: Reversal*

Another type of transformation takes place when a riddle metaphor is reversed. If the original metaphor says "A = B", the new metaphor states "B = A". Reversibility is peculiar to poetic metaphors, perhaps indeed essential for their 'freshness'. In Finnish riddles, the reversal mechanism is surprisingly productive.

I will now present a series of transformations of the reversed counterpart of riddle (1):

(8) *Mamsseli kasvoi mäen päällä*
hiukset hartioilla. — Koivu. 375/6
'A virgin grew on a hill
her hair hanging on her shoulders. — Birch tree.'

Transformation 1; transformer "decorates herself" →

(9) *Talvella on vaatteeton,*
kesällä kantaa uuden morsiuspuvun. — Lehtipuu. 374/2
'In the winter is naked,
in the summer wears a new bridal dress. — Leaf tree.'

Another one, identical riddle states the same situation:

(10) *Morsian mäellä seisoo*
kesät kaiket kauniina,
talvella aivan alasti. — Lehtipuu. 374/1
'A bride stands on a hill
all summer beautiful,
in the winter, stark naked. — Leaf tree.'

Transformation 2, "gives birth" →

(11) *Keväällä on korea morsian,*
syksyllä lapsia synnyttää,
lapset kaikki ympyriäisiä
ja kullakin kivi vatsassa. — Tuomi kukkineen, marjoineen. 378
'In the spring is a beautiful bride,
in the fall gives birth to children,
the children are all round
and each has a stone in his stomach. — *Tuomi* (wildcherry) with its flowers, berries.'

Transformation 3, transformer "loses family" (and transformation 4, transformer "renews itself") →

(12) *Syksyn leski, talven leski,*
suvella uusi morsian. — Lehtipuu. 374/4
'A widow all autumn, a widow all winter,
in the summer, a new bride. — Leaf tree.'

Trees are like women, yet they have in addition to their life cycle also their annual cycle of blossoming, ripening of fruits, and their loss.
The second series of transformations can be mapped :

I	II	III	IV	V
maiden	grows	hairs	?branches? leaves	birch tree

transformation 1, transformer "is decorated" →

bride		bridal dress	leaves, flowers	tree

transformation 2, transformer "gives birth" →

woman		children	berries	wild cherry tree

transformation 3, transformer "loses family" →

woman		widowhood	winter	tree

Comparing series I of transformations to this reversed series one can see that many, but not all transformations have their reversed counterpart. All the general themes are there : the beauty of youth, the fertility of mature age, and the view of old age as deprived. But the fit of woodpecker/tree = nursing child/mother was not tight enough to be generative.

We can write out a series of analogy formulas if we assign values to the elements of the riddle structures analyzed above. The order of the columns (I-V) in the tabulations is from the signans ('core' of the riddle image), *i.e.,* the Given Term, (I) through the Given Constant Premiss (II), and the juxtaposition of the Hidden Variable Premiss (III) and Given Variable Premiss (IV) to the discovery of the Hidden Term (V), which is the answer. The original connection is a leap which sees all growing things as members of one set. This analogy could be described :

growing : trees : : growing : human beings
II : I : : II : V

Or, if we wish to assign the values

x = growing
A = tree
B = human being

$$x : A : : x : B$$

But this is obviously a summary statement, paradox-like, and must be immediately specified. Already riddle (1) has conditioned the underlying analogy by reference to roots and rootlessness; that is III : I : : IV : V. We can continue to list elements of the following riddles :

a = twigs?	b = hair
a_1 = leaves, flowers	b_1 = bridal dress
a_2 = berries	b_2 = child (before birth)
a_3 = branches	b_3 = child (at birth)
a_4 = "dependants" = birds	b_4 = child (nursing)
a_5 = death = loss of roots	b_5 = death (loss of fertility)

We can now write the whole series of transformations as :

$t_1[a/A = b/B] \rightarrow a_1/A = b_1/B$ (riddles 1 to 2)
$t_2[a_1/A = b_1/B] \rightarrow a_2/A = b_2/B$ (riddles 2 to 3)
$t_3[a_2/A = b_2/B] \rightarrow a_3/A = b_3/B$ (riddle 3 to 4 and 5)
$t_4[a_3/A = b_3/B] \rightarrow a_4/A = b_4/B$ (riddles 4 and 5 to 6)

Until this point, it seems necessary to consider the transformations a chain, for (ideally) a woman is not made pregnant before being wed, does not give birth before being pregnant, and cannot nurse without giving birth. But for the next transformation, there is a choice of rules : either

$$t_5[a/A = b/B] \rightarrow a_5/A = b_5/B \text{ (riddle 1 to 7)}$$

or

$$t_5[a_4/A = b_4/B] \rightarrow a_5/A = b_5/B \text{ (riddle 6 to 7).}$$

We have so far considered the metaphors which compare a woman to a tree. Now to the reversed series, starting with riddle (8). Is that a true reversal of (1), with only the sex specification added? It seems to presuppose a riddle as we have interpreted riddle (1) here, in which a woman would be compared to a leaf tree. But the reference to the "hairs on her shoulders" (in Finnish *hiukset,* a plural form, instead of another possibility *tukka,* a singular form) evokes also the mention of roots as a mirror picture: as roots grow down from the bottom, so hairs grow up from the top. A little reluctantly, recognizing that the fit is not perfect, we will note the reversed transformation (T_r) with the transformer t_r (reversal).

$$t_r[a/A = b/B] \rightarrow b/B = a/A \text{ (riddle 1 to 8).}$$

From this, we get the next riddle

$$t_1[b/B = a/A] \rightarrow b_1/B = a_1/A \text{ (riddle 8 to 9, 10 and beginning of 11, which is a complex riddle).}$$

However, this riddle can also be considered a result of a reversal operation:

$$t_r[a_1/A = b_1/B] \rightarrow b_1/B = a_1/A \text{ (riddle 2 to 9 and 10).}$$

The remaining two riddles correspond a little diffusely to the 'Tree-Woman' series. It is arbitrary to choose either t_2 or t_3 of that riddle as a counterpart; both fit partially and only partially.

$$t_2[b_1/B = a_1/A] \rightarrow b_2/B = a_2/A \text{ (riddles 9 and 10 to 11).}$$

And, finally, acknowledging the gap in the materials:

$$t_5[b/B = a/A] \rightarrow b_5/B = a_5/A \text{ (riddle 8 to 12).}$$

I believe to have established the rules of the game; variations can be found (riddle 9 to 12; riddle 10 to 12, riddle 11 to 12 are all possible transformations). I will now map the correspondence:

Tree-Woman	Woman-Tree
1	8
2	9, 10, 11a
3	
4,5	11b
6	
7	12

4.3 *Transformations, Series III; IV: Complementary Sets; Inversion*

The above series includes a metaphor, its 'analysis' or scrutiny by riddle posers to investigate how far it can be stretched, its reversal, and an investigation how far the reversals are possible. The riddle is put to play until all the possibilities of the image have been exhausted.

However, other members are contained by the original sets: there are other trees than leaf trees, and there are other human beings than women. The set "women" needs a complement "men" to fill the universe "humans", and, in the Finnish way of seeing a forest, the set "leaf trees" has the complement "needle trees" *(havupuu)*; together they form the universe of "trees". These possibilities are indeed realized, and there are comparisons of men and trees in metaphors. These metaphors, however, are not used to build riddles, but proverbs, and the evidence is too scarce to analyze them in depth.

Men like pines (Kuusi [ed.], 1960: 383)
Men like trees in the forest (Kuusi [ed.], 1960: 386)
Black and crooked like a swamp spruce (Kuusi [ed.], 1960: 398)[9].

In these proverbs of comparison *(vertaussananparsi)* the image is the tree and the 'answer' the man. These examples, insufficient as they are, serve to point out a connection between riddle structures and proverb structures: whereas in riddles, the answerer has to work his way through the structure (in the order of elements I-II-III-IV) to find the signatum (V), in proverbs the signatum is provided by the context, the situation (such as looking at a group of men). The 'answer' is observed, and the image is then provided. The structure of the comparison is similar, and can be identical, but the process of communication (the unfolding of the message) is reversed.

[9] These examples are from Matti Kuusi (ed.), *Suomen kansan vertauksia*, pp. 383, 386, 298.

If we allow for *pars pro toto,* we have riddles based on this expected analogy :

$$\underline{\bar{a}}/\bar{A} = \bar{b}/\bar{B}$$

which can provisorily be read :
needles/*havupuu,* evergreen tree = masculine attributes/man.

(13) *Katajikko kannon päässä*
liikkuu tuulella, tyynelläkin. — *Parta.* 10/1
'A juniper bush on a stump
moves in wind and calm. — Beard.'

(14) *Katajikko niemen päässä*
tuhisevi tuulettakin. — *Miehen parta.* 10/2
'A juniper bush on a point
rustles without wind. — Man's beard.'

(15) *Kataja mäellä kasvaa*
tyvi ylös-, latva alaspäin. — *Parta.* 10/3.
'A juniper grows on a hill
with the bottom upwards, top downwards. — Beard.'

As I pointed out above, the metonymic skewing prevents this from being commensurable with the other riddle images considered so far, and I quote these riddles only to underline the equation between evergreens and masculinity.

For $\bar{b}/\bar{B} = \underline{\bar{a}}/\bar{A}$, there are riddles :

(16) *Hiitta, hiitta,*
sininen viitta,
parta pitkin naamaa. — *Kuusi.* 373/1
'[nonsense rhyme]
a blue mantle,
his beard covers his face. — Spruce.'

(17) *Tirkki, tarkki tattarlainen*
liepehiään lieputtaa. — *Katajapehko.* 374
'[nonce] a tartar
swaying the hem [of his mantle]. — Juniper bush.'

(18) *Talvella takki päällä,*
kesällä liinapaidallaan. — *Petäjä, josta on koluttu leiväksi kuorta.* 372/12

'In the winter, he has a coat on,
in the summer, he is in a linen shirt. — Pine whose bark is being used for bread [*ersatz* in times of famine].'

(19) *Mies seisoo sepelissä*
hattu päässä kallellaan,
kylkiluut kymärässä. — Kartanon kuusi. 373/2
'A man stands with a jacket [?] on,
his hat on his head askew,
his sides [lit. ribs] bent. — Spruce of farmyard.'

(20) *Sotamies mäellä seisoo,*
sadalla sapelilla varustettu. — Havupuu. 371
'A soldier stands on a hill
armed with a hundred swords. — Evergreen.'

(21) *Iso mies, harjaspää,*
pojat kaikki kaksosia. — Mänty. 372/11
'A big man, a brushy hair,
all sons are twins. — Pine.'

(22) *Mies kasvoi, tukka liehui,*
mies kuoli, mato jäyti,
jaloista kansaa kasvoi. — Puu. 369/5
'A man grew, his hair swayed [in the wind],
the man died, a worm chewed,
at his feet, new people grew. — Tree.'

Whereas the leaves of a tree were repeatedly compared to the bridal dress of a woman, the "needles" of evergreens are compared to more lasting garments of men. In this our last group of riddles (13-22), we thus have at least our transformer$_1$ in operation (and now it seems badly worded, for "being decorated" seems indeed offending to the masculinity principle). Then what of the following transformers which were labelled "is fertilized", "reproduces", and "feeds its dependent"? The 'masculine' riddles refer to having offspring but do not dwell on its biological aspects. Further, it would seem natural to consider authority the complement of the nursing function. Riddle (20) depicts a soldier with a hundred swords; and, although the transformation trespasses some of our borders otherwise, the following riddle gives an amusing picture of "anti-nursing":

(23) *Pojat kaikki vapisevat*
vaikk' on isä ääneti. — Haavan lehdet. 377
'All the sons tremble,
although the father is silent. — The leaves of a trembling poplar *(haapa)*.'

Here we have an interesting result of a conflict : leaf trees are feminine, but — one has to resolve the problem of authority being masculine. A parallel conflict has made the following riddle 'feminine' :

(24) *Tuhannen vuoden vanha ämmä*
joka vuosi lapsen tekee. — Honka ja käpy. 373
'An old woman *(ämmä)*, a thousand years old has a child every year. — Pine and cone.'

It is impossible for a man to give birth; but pine trees are masculine. The dilemma is solved by stripping the woman of all her femininity : it is twice denied, by the word *ämmä* 'old woman', and by the emphasis on her age, a thousand years old.

To make the series symmetrical with the previous, we should switch the order of 2 and 3; but they can also be considered independent transformations, without any necessary mutual order (and indeed fit the ethnography better as ordered here). It only remains now to formalize the transformations :

First, the elements :

$\bar{a}$ = moss (on bark) — $\bar{b}$ = beard
$\bar{a}_1$ = needles — $\bar{b}_1$ = permanent garments
$\bar{a}_2$ = cones — $\bar{b}_2$ = child (of man)
$\bar{a}_3$ = branches — $\bar{b}_3$ = swords
$\bar{a}_4$ = descendants (sprouts) — $\bar{b}_4$ = descendants (non-nursing)
$\bar{a}_5$ = death (loss of roots) — $\bar{b}_5$ = death

We can now consider riddle (16) the complement of riddle (8); transformer t_i(inversion) :

$$ti[b/B = a/A] \rightarrow \bar{b}/\bar{B} = \bar{a}/\bar{A} \text{ (riddle 8 to 16)}$$

The rest of the riddles can be seen as expansions of the new metaphor :

$t_1[\bar{b}/\bar{B} = \bar{a}/\bar{A}] \rightarrow \bar{b}_1/\bar{B} = \bar{a}_1/\bar{A}$ (riddle 16 to second part of 16 and 17, 18, 19)
$t_2[\bar{b}/\bar{B} = \bar{a}/\bar{A}] \rightarrow \bar{b}_2/\bar{B} = \bar{a}_2/\bar{A}$ (riddle 16 to 21)
$t_3[\bar{b}/\bar{B} = \bar{a}/\bar{A}] \rightarrow \bar{b}_3/\bar{B} = \bar{a}_3/\bar{A}$ (riddle 16 to 20)
$t_{4,5}[\bar{b}/\bar{B} = \bar{a}/\bar{A}] \rightarrow (\bar{b}_4/\bar{B} = \bar{a}_4/\bar{A}) + (\bar{b}_5/\bar{B} = \bar{a}_5/\bar{A})$ (riddle 16 to 22).

Tentatively, I map the transformations :

I	II	III	IV	V
man	grows	beard	moss on bark	evergreen

transformation 1, transformer "is dressed" →

man		mantle	needles	juniper, pine, spruce

transformation 2, transformer "is armed" (aggression, authority) →

soldier		swords	branches	evergreen

transformation 3, transformer "has offspring" →

man		sons	cones	pine

transformation 4, transformer "dies" →

man		"worm chewed"	falling	tree

The formalizations above are intended to show the processes by which the riddle-poser builds new riddles. I have simplified some; more than one have the form of the last, where two transformations take place simultaneously (or as if). I have privileged the main elements and considered the compound riddles which I have even in this small corpus as simple. Finer analysis is possible, but in my opinion it would have to be in the same vein as already done here, and therefore further demonstration seems unnecessary.

It remains now only to sum up the series of transformations that lead to the construction of each riddle in the corpus discussed.

First, it is possible to present by a diagram the 'ring' of transformations which takes place starting with the basic metaphor A : : B. It goes as follows :

$\boxed{A :: B} \rightarrow \boxed{B :: A} \rightarrow \boxed{\bar{B} :: \bar{A}} \rightarrow \boxed{\bar{A} :: \bar{B}} \; [\rightarrow \boxed{A :: B} \rightarrow]$

inversion reversal inversion reversal inversion

And, in detail, each riddle is derivable from the others in the following manner :

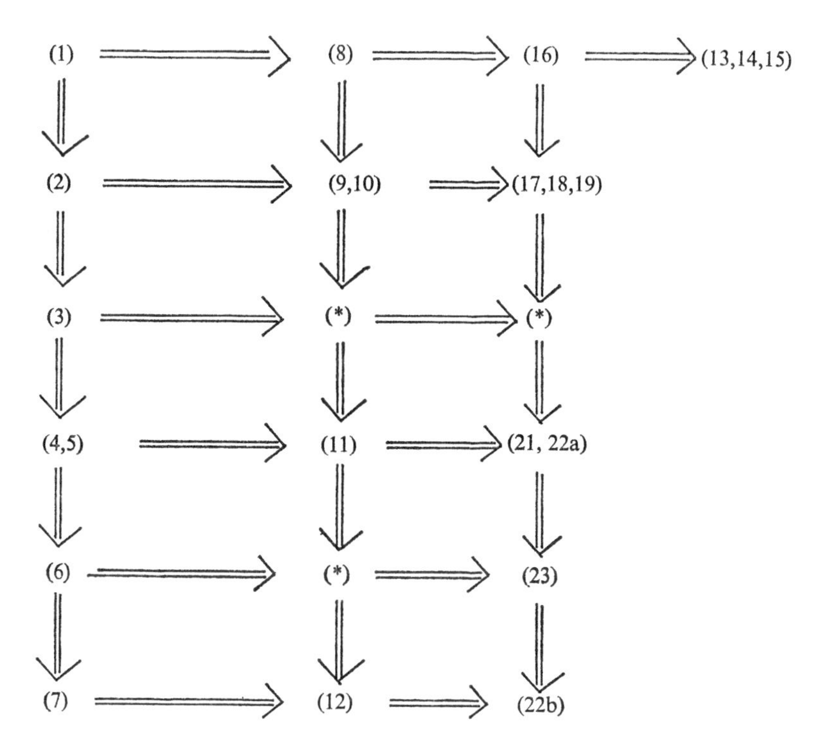

In another paper (Köngäs Maranda, 1970 a) I have done the same mapping with a somewhat finer technique; the only thing to emphasize here is that in this way, one can show what alternative chains of transformations yield a given transform starting with a given kernel riddle.

5. CONCLUSION

The process of riddle building is a mental process and one we can discover only through an investigation of its product, the riddle. The riddle transformations discussed above are mechanisms by which the classifications of a language can be reexamined by the speakers of the language, by those who share the classifications. The paring of classes (or sets, as I have used the word above) creates kernel riddles; this first pairing is in our example, and perhaps often otherwise, in the form of a paradox. But once some similarity has been shown to exist between two sets, expansions and reversals and expansions of the reversals are easy to predict and easy to build.

There is a riddle form which in a sense is a 'meta-riddle' : the question "What is the difference between A and B?" To this, the answer is "I do not know", and the answerer receives a retort which puts him to shame. ("What is the difference between the behind of a horse and a mailbox? — I do not know. — Then you should not take letters to a mailbox.") The question can be read : Can you make a riddle metaphor of A and B?

Riddles are pre-established, coded including the answer. This does not mean that they are mechanically memorized. The variety of forms of one basic riddle, found in all traditions, convinces me of the fact that people do not learn and memorize riddles but riddle-making rules. It may well be that even two identical variants are identical only because they are made of the same elements using the same rules, not because one is a repetition of the other by the route of memorizing.

If in the preceding I have been able to discover true mechanisms of riddle making, then I should be able to predict riddles. The rules do, indeed, provide possibilities of predicting. However, an interesting problem remains : if one predicts a riddle that cannot be found, is this proof that the rules are after all faulty?

To me the answer is no. The rules will also be valid if they predict correct riddles, disregarding if anyone has yet constructed them in the culture or not. The situation is directly comparable to that of phonemics (or syntactic theory) : if one has correctly identified the phonemes of a language and their combinatorics, he will predict 'correctly' even if a word he builds is NOT YET used in the language. Exhaustive generative rules can generate — for example — the following words for Finnish :

katu 'street'
satu 'märchen'
latu 'ski track'
**matu*
**natu* etc.

and they will be valid despite the fact that the starred two last words are not realized.

But, in contrast, the rules would not be valid, if they generated

> **sratu, *pratu, *platu, *ksatu,* etc.

If we thus see a Finnish riddle

> *Pappi istuu tien vieress'*
> *valkoinen kraiji kaulass'. — Virstantolppa.* 295/3
> 'Priest is sitting on the roadside
> with a white tie on his neck. — Milestone',

then we can predict that there will be a reversal in which a milestone is depicted in the pulpit.

> *Mustaselkä tien viitta;*
> *kun nousee ylös,*
> *alkaa hyrsätä ja härsätä. — Pappi kirkossa.* 321/24.
> 'A milestone with a black back:
> it climbs up
> to snort and chort. — Priest in the church.'

At least to an extent, we can also predict that since 'priest' as well as 'milestone' are sets which lack complements, we will not find inversion in operation here.

In the preceding, the two universes compared were that of trees and that of humans. For trees, we found a set "leaf trees" and its complement "evergreens"; for humans, the set "women" and the complement "men" (the order is given by the importance of each in riddles, and reflects no other ideology). These can create four series of riddles:

I $A = B$
II $B = A$
III $\bar{A} = \bar{B}$
IV $\bar{B} = \bar{A}$

However, only I, II, and IV were in fact found. Series III thus remains a possible, but not realized series of riddles in Finnish folklore. (Further collecting might uncover the riddles, for they are 'natural riddles' for Finnish tradition).

In the preceding, I have established some rules of riddle building which can be put thus:

1. Riddles are metaphors which establish, on the basis of an initial insight (which is largely unpredictable and has a 'poetic' function) the equivalence of two sets. These sets are commonly objects, either cultural or natural, or living beings, such as humans or animals, domesticated or wild.

2. The greater the initial opposition between the two sets, the more effective the riddle metaphor. Thus it is more striking to compare sets in double opposition, such as wild animals and cultural objects; but for a riddle, any accepted classification serves as a starting point. 'Riddlers' are eager to 'break' any classifications that come their way.

3. The initial insight is based on the identity of one function (*i.e.*, one element) shared by the two sets.

4. The very simplest riddles could perhaps be considered comparable to kernel sentences. They consist of four expressed parts: the two sets compared, which can be called two terms; the common function or element which can be called the true premiss, and a false premiss, an element which is not true of the term of the riddle image but which fits the term of the riddle answer; additionally, a fifth part, a hidden premiss is implied.

5. The discovery of the coded answer consists of noting the false premiss and discovering a term for which the premiss will be true. If several such terms are found, the riddle will have several correct answers.

6. Transformations of riddles are effected through the investigation of the two sets A and B and the discovery of elements ($a_1a_2 \ldots a_n$; $b_1b_2 \ldots b_n$) which can be compared. The transformer then becomes the true premiss, and the more common true premisses are found the more riddle transformations can be built, until all the similarities are exhausted.

7. Riddle making can thus be seen as a systematic investigation of the 'native classifications' of any culture.

8. A peculiarity of riddle metaphors is that they are reversible $T_i(A = B) \rightarrow B = A$. In this respect, riddle metaphors differ from the common metaphors of the language and in their openness resemble other poetic metaphors, although they are usually more conventional than 'free' poetic metaphors. The reversibility of riddle metaphors seems to vary cross-culturally.

9. If each of the sets compared has a well-defined complementary set, then inversion can be expected to take place, and still another type of transformation can be found:

$$T_1(A = B) \rightarrow \bar{A} = \bar{B}$$

10. The generative power of the above rules is such that knowing the classifications of a culture one can predict all possible (acceptable) riddles. If all the possibilities were exhausted, the number of riddles created would, however, be greater than the number of riddles in the culture; for it seems certain that, as with linguistic forms (*e.g.,* words), a culture does not realize all the possibilities. This is a hypothesis which is almost impossible to verify, for riddles are a relatively large form (linguistically), and it is therefore not easy to collect all riddles of a culture; it can also be remembered that if the riddling rules are still operative in a culture, new riddles can be created any time. For the validity of the rules established here, it is only important to see if the rules cover all riddles found.

BIBLIOGRAPHY

Aarne, Antti, and Stith Thompson,
1961 *The Types of the Folktales* (= Folklore Fellows Communications 184), (Helsinki).
Anon.,
1949 "Climax of Relations", in Maria Leach (ed.), *Standard Dictionary of Folklore, Mythology, and Legend* I (New York), 236.
Aristotle,
Poetics.
Categories.
Armstrong, Robert Plant,
1959 "Content Analysis in Folkloristics", in Ithiel de Sola Pool (ed.), *Trends in Content Analysis* (Urbana, Ill.), 151-170.
Balys, Jonas,
1958 *Lietuvin dainos amerikeje* [Lithuanian folksongs in America], (Boston).
Ben-Amos, D.,
1963 "The Situation Structure of the Non-Humorous English Ballad", *Midwest Folklore* XIII, 163-176.
Bouteiller, Marcelle,
1958-59 "Cosmologie et médecine magique selon notre folklore rural : Esquisse d'analyse structurale", *L'Ethnographie* N.S. LIII, 91-95.
Bremond, Claude,
1964 "Le message narratif", *Communications* 4, 4-32.
1966 "La logique des possibles narratifs", *Communications* 8, 60-76.
1968 "La postérité américaine de Propp", *Communications* 11, 148-164.
Buchler, Ira R., and Henry A. Selby,
1968 *A Formal Study of Myth* (Austin, the University of Texas Center for Inter-cultural Studies in Folklore).
Campbell, Joseph,
1949 *The Hero with a Thousand Faces* (New York, 3rd printing 1960).
Child, Francis James,
1882-1898 *English and Scottish Popular Ballads*, 5 vols. (reprinted in New York, 1956).
Chomsky, Noam,
1962 *Syntactic Structures* ('s-Gravenhage, 2nd printing).
Delarue, Paul,
1957 *Le conte populaire français* I (Paris).
Dundes, Alan,
1961 "Brown County Superstitions", *Midwest Folklore* XI, 25-56.
1962 "From Etic to Emic Units in the Structural Study of Folktales", *Journal of American Folklore* LXXV, 95-105.

1962 "The Binary Structure of 'Unsuccessful Repetition' in Lithuanian Folk Tales", *Western Folklore* XXI (July), 165-174.
1962 "Trends in Content Analysis: A Review Article", *Midwest Folklore* XII, 31-38.
1964 "The Morphology of North-American Indian Folktales", *Folklore Fellows Communications* 195 (Helsinki).
1970 "The Making and Breaking of Friendship as a Structural Frame in African Folktales", in Pierre Maranda and Elli Köngäs Maranda (eds.), *Structural Analysis of Oral Tradition*, (Philadelphia, University of Pennsylvania Press, in press).

Dundes, Alan, Edmond R. Leach, Pierre Maranda, and David Maybury-Lewis,
1970 "An Experiment: Notes and Queries from the Desk, With a Reply by the Ethnographer", in Pierre Maranda and Elli Köngäs Maranda (eds.), *Structural Analysis of Oral Tradition.*

Durant, Gilbert,
1960 *Les structures anthropologiques de l'imaginaire* (Paris, Presses Universitaires de France).

Eliade, Mircea,
1953 *Traité d'histoire des religions* (Paris).

Erixon, Sigurd,
1937 "Introduction", *Folkliv* I, 5-12.

Finlands svenska folkdiktning,
1917 I A, *Sagor* [Swedish folklore of Finland, I A, *sage*] I (Helsingfors).

Fisher, J.L.,
1963 "The Sociopsychological Analysis of Folktales", *Current Anthropology* 4, 235-295.

Georges, Robert A., and Alan Dundes,
1963 "Toward a Structural Definition of the Riddle", *Journal of American Folklore* LXXVI, 111-118.

Greimas, A. Julien,
1966a *Sémantique structurale* (Paris, Larousse).
1966b "Éléments pour une théorie de l'interprétation du récit mythique", *(Recherches sémiologiques)*, *Communications* 8, 28-59.
1970 "The Interpretation of Myth: Theory and Practice", in Pierre Maranda and Elli Köngäs Maranda (eds.), *Structural Analysis of Oral Tradition.*

Haavio, Martti,
1952a *Kirjokansi* [An anthology of epic poetry], (Helsinki.)
1952b *Laulupuu* [An anthology of lyric poetry], (Helsinki).

Haavio, Martti, and Jouko Hautala (eds.),
1946 *Suomen kansan arvoituskirja* [Book of riddles of the Finnish people], (Helsinki, facsimile 4th impression 1957).

Halstead, W.C.,
1960 "Thinking, Imagery, and Memory", in J. Field *et al.* (eds.), *Handbook of Physiology, Section I: Neurophysiology* II, III (Washington).

Herskovits, Melville J.,
1949 "Folklore", in Maria Leach (ed.), *Dictionary of Folklore, Mythology, and Legend* I (New York), 400.

Honko, Lauri,
1959 "Luonnonjärjestyksen palauttamisen aate parannusriiteissä" [The principle of the restoration of the cosmic order in healing rites], in Pertti Virtaranta, Terho Itkonen, and Paavo Pulkkinen (eds.), *Verba docent: Juhlakirja Lauri Hakulisen 60-vuotispaiväksi 6. 10. 1959* [Verba docent: Festschrift for Lauri Hakulinen's 60th birthday 6. 10. 1959], (Helsinki), 599-613.

Hymes, Dell,
1970 "The 'Wife' Who 'Goes Out' like a Man : Reinterpretation of a Clackamas Chinook Myth", in Pierre Maranda and Elli Köngäs Maranda (eds.), *Structural Analysis of Oral Tradition.*
Jakobson, Roman,
1956 "Two Aspects of Language and Two Types of Aphasic Disturbances", in Roman Jakobson and Morris Halle, *Fundamentals of Language* (The Hague), 55-82.
Jakobson, Roman, and Morris Halle,
1956 *Fundamentals of Language* (The Hague, Mouton).
Jakobson, Roman, and Claude Lévi-Strauss,
1962 "'Le Chat' de Charles Baudelaire", *L'Homme* II, 5-21.
Jensen, Ad. E.,
1951 *Mythos und Kult bei Naturvölkern* (Wiesbaden).
Kluckhohn, Clyde,
1958 "The Scientific Study of Values", *3 Lectures* (Toronto).
Köhler, Wolfgang,
1959 *Gestalt Psychology* (New York).
Köngäs, Elli-Kaija,
1960 "The Earth-Diver (Th. A 812)", *Ethnohistory* VII, 151-180.
1962 "A Finnish Schwank Pattern : The Farmer-Servant Cycle of the Kuusisto Family", *Midwest Folklore* XI, 197-211.
Köngäs Maranda, Elli,
1963a "The Concept of Folklore", *Midwest Folklore* XIII (1963), 69-88.
1963b *Finnish-American Folklore*, University Microfilm, Ann Arbor, Michigan.
1965 "Myth and Art as Teaching Materials", (= *Educational Services, Inc., Occasional Paper* 5), (Cambridge, Mass.).
1966a "What Does a Myth Tell about a Society?", *Radcliffe Institute Seminars, Jan. 1966*, ms.
1966b "Two Tales of Orphans", *Radcliffe Seminars, Feb. 1966*, ms.
1969 "Structure des énigmes", *L'Homme:* 3, 5-48.
1970a "Perinteen transformaatiosääntöjen tutkimisesta", *Virittäjä* 2 (1970), 277-292.
1970b "The Logic of Riddles", in Pierre Maranda and Elli Köngäs Maranda (eds.), *Structural Analysis of Oral Tradition.*
Kuusi, Matti,
1958 "Omaistenvertailukertaus" *Kalevalaseuran vuosikirja* XXXVIII (Helsinki), 89-108.
1962 "Kansanparadokseista" *Kalevalaseuran vuosikirja* XLII (Helsinki), 56-68.
Kuusi, Matti (ed.),
1960 *Suomen kansan vertauksia* (Helsinki).
Labov, William, and Joshua Waletzky,
1967 "Narrative Analysis : Oral Versions of Personal Experience", in June Helm (ed.), *Essays on the Verbal and Visual Arts: Proceedings of the 1966 Annual Spring Meeting of the American Ethnological Society* (Seattle and London), 12-44.
Leach, Edmund A.,
1961 "Lévi-Strauss in the Garden of Eden : An Examination of Some Recent Developments in the Analysis of Myth", *Transactions of the New York Academy of Sciences*, Series II, XXIII, 386-396.
1962 "Genesis as Myth", *Discovery* (May), 30-35, reprinted in John Middleton (ed.), *Myth and Cosmos*; *Readings in Mythology and Symbolism* (New York, 1967), 1-13.

1966 "The Legitimacy of Solomon: Some Structural Aspects of Old Testament History", *European Journal of Sociology* 7, 58-101.
1970 "*Kimil:* A Category of Andamanese Thought", in Pierre Maranda and Elli Köngäs Maranda (eds.), *Structural Analysis of Oral Tradition.*

Leach, Edmund A. (ed.),
1967 *The Structural Study of Myth and Totemism* (= *A.S.A. Monographs* 5), (London).

Lévi-Strauss, Claude,
1949 *Les structures élémentaires de la parenté* (Paris).
1953 "Social Structure", in A.L. Kroeber, *Anthropology Today* (Chicago).
1955 "The Structural Study of Myth", *Journal of American Folklore* LXVIII, 428-444, reprinted in Thomas A. Sebeok (ed.), *Myth: A Symposium* (= *Midland Book* MB 83), (Bloomington, 1965), 81-106.
1958 *Anthropologie structurale* (Paris).
1959 "La Geste d'Asdiwal", Extrait de *L'Annuaire 1958-59* (Paris, École Pratique des Hautes Études, Section des Sciences Religieuses), 3-43. English translation in Edmund Leach (ed.), *The Structural Study of Myth and Totemism,* 1-47.
1960a Collège de France, chaire d'anthropologie sociale, Leçon inaugurale faite le mardi 5 janvier 1960 (Paris), partly reprinted under the title 1960c.
1960b "Problèmes de l'invariance en anthropologie", *Diogène* XXXI, 23-33.
1960c "Four Winnebago Myths: A Structural Sketch", in Stanley Diamond (ed.), *Culture in History* (New York), 351-362, reprinted in John Middleton (ed.), *Myth and Cosmos: Readings in Mythology and Symbolism* (New York, 1967), 15-26.
1960d "La structure et la forme", *Cahiers de l'institut de science économique appliquée* IXC, Série M.N. 7, 3-36, also under the title 1960e.
1960e "L'analyse morphologique des contes populaires russes", *International Journal of Slavic Poetics and Linguistics*, 122-249.
1962 *La pensée sauvage* (Paris).
1964 *Le cru et le cuit: Mythologiques* I (Paris).
1966 *Du miel aux cendres: Mythologiques* II (Paris).
1968 *L'origine des manières de table: Mythologiques* III (Paris).
1970 "The Deduction of the Crane", in Pierre Maranda, and Elli Köngäs Maranda (eds.), *Structural Analysis of Oral Tradition.*

Maranda, Pierre,
1963 "Note sur l'élément de parenté", *Anthropos* 58, 810-828.
1965 "The Structural Study of Myth", Lecture Given at Harvard University.
1967a "Computers in the Bush: Tools for the Automatic Analysis of Myths", in June Helm (ed.), *Essays on the Verbal and Visual Arts: Proceedings of the 1966 Annual Spring Meetings of the American Ethnological Society* (Seattle and London), 77-83.
1967b "Formal Analysis and Intra-Cultural Studies", *Social Science Information* 6, 7-36.
1968 "Analyse qualitative et quantitative de mythes sur ordinateurs", in J.C. Gardin and B. Jaulin (eds.), *Calcul et formalisation dans les sciences de l'homme* (Paris), 79-86.
1971 "Anthropological Analytics: Lévi-Strauss' Concept of Social Structure", in H. Nutini and I. Buchler (eds.), *The Anthropology of Claude Lévi-Strauss* (New York).

Maranda, Pierre, and Elli Köngäs Maranda (eds.),
1970 *Structural Analysis of Oral Tradition* (Philadelphia).

Matta, Roberto da,
1970 "Myth and Anti-Myth among the Timbira", in Pierre Maranda and Elli Köngäs Maranda (eds.), *Structural Analysis of Oral Tradition.*
Morin, Violette,
1966 "L'histoire drôle", *Communications* 8, 102-119.
Needham, Rodney,
1960 "A Structural Analysis of Aimol Society", *Bijdragen tot de Taal-, Land- en Volkenkunde* CXVI, 103-104.
Osgood, Charles,
1959 "The Representational Model and Relevant Research Methods", in Ithiel de Sola Pool (ed.), *Trends in Content Analysis* (Urbana, Ill.), 33-88.
Peacock, James L.
1970 "Class, Clown, and Cosmology in Javanese Drama : An Analysis of Symbolic and Social Action", in Pierre Maranda and Elli Köngäs Maranda (eds.), *Structural Analysis of Oral Tradition.*
Piaget, Jean,
1945 *La formation du symbole chez l'enfant* (Paris).
1947 *La psychologie de l'intelligence* (Paris).
1958 *Les relations entre l'intelligence et l'affectivité dans le développement mental de l'enfant* (Paris).
Pool, Ithiel de Sola (ed.),
1959 *Trends in Content Analysis* (Urbana, Ill.).
Pouillon, Jean,
1966 "L'analyse des mythes", *L'Homme* VI : 1, 100-105.
Powlinson, P. S.,
1965 "A Paragraph Analysis of a Yagua Folktale", *International Journal of American Linguistics* 31, 109-118.
Propp, Vladimir,
1958 *Morphology of the Folktale*, ed. by Svatava Pirkova-Jakobson, transl. Laurence Scott (= *Publication Ten of the Indiana University Research Center in Anthropology, Folklore, and Linguistics*) (Bloomington).
1965 "Les transformations des contes fantastiques", in T. Todorov (ed.), Théorie de la littérature (Paris), 234-262.
Rasmussen, Knud,
1931 *The Netsilik Eskimos: Social Life and Spiritual Culture* (= *Report of the Fifth Thule Expedition, 1921-1924* VIII (Köpenhagen).
Richard, Philippe,
1967 "Analyse des *Mythologiques* de Claude Lévi-Strauss", *L'Homme et la Société*, 109-133, and 1969, 179-191.
Richer, Ernest,
1961 "Un instrument de description formelle des langues : la théorie des *lieux linguistiques*", *Revue de l'Association canadienne de Linguistique* VI : 3, 192-208.
1962 *Lieux linguistiques et latin classique* (Montréal).
Saporta, Sol, and Thomas A. Sebeok,
1959 "Linguistics and Content Analysis", in Ithiel de Sola Pool (ed.), *Trends in Content Analysis* (Urbana, Ill.), 131-150.
Saussure, Ferdinand de,
1916 *Cours de linguistique générale* (Paris).
Scott, Charles T.,
Persian and Arabic Riddles: A Language-Centered Approach to Genre Definition. (*Supplement, International Journal of American Linguistics* 31: 4, part II).

Sebeok, Thomas A.,
1950 "Cheremis Dream Portents", *Southwestern Journal of Anthropology* VI, 273-285.
1953 "The Structure and Content of Cheremis Charms", *Anthropos* XLVIII, 369-388.
1956 "Sound and Meaning in a Cheremis Folksong Text", in Morris Halle, Horace G. Lunt, Hugh McLean, and Cornelis van Schooneveld (eds.), *For Roman Jakobson* (The Hague), 430-439.
1959 "Folksong Viewed as Code and Message", *Anthropos* LIV, 141-153.
1960 "Decoding a Text: Levels and Aspects in a Cheremis Sonnet", in Thomas A. Sebeok (ed.), *Style in Language* (New York), 221-235.
Sebeok, Thomas A., and Louis H. Orzack,
1953 "The Structure and Content of Cheremis Charms", Part II, *Anthropos* XLVIII, 760-772.
Sebeok, Thomas A., and Frances J. Ingemann,
1956 *Studies in Cheremis: The Supernatural* (= *Viking Fund Publications in Anthropology* 22), (New York).
Sebeok, Thomas A. (ed.),
1965 *Myth: A Symposium* (= *Midland Book* MB83), (Bloomington and London).
Simonsuuri, Lauri (ed.),
1947 *Myytillisiä tarinoita* [Mythical *sagen*], (Helsinki).
1961 *Typen- und Motivverzeichnis der finnischen mythischen Sagen* (= *Folklore Fellows Communications* 182), (Helsinki).
Sperber, Dan,
1968 "Le structuralisme en anthropologie", in Oswald Ducrot, Tzvetan Todorov, Dan Sperber, Moustafa Safouan, and François Wahl, *Qu'est-ce que le structuralisme?* (Paris), 167-238.
Sturtevant, Edgar H.,
1960 *An Introduction to Linguistic Science* (New Haven).
Suomen Kansan Vanhat Runot
1908-1948 [The Ancient Poems of the Finnish People], 33 vols. (Helsinki).
Taylor, Archer,
1951 *English Riddles from Oral Tradition* (Berkeley and Los Angeles).
Tesnière, Lucien,
1959 *Éléments de syntaxe structurale* (Paris).
Turner, Victor,
1970 "The Syntax of Symbolism in a Ndembu Ritual", in Pierre Maranda and Elli Köngäs Maranda (eds.), *Structural Analysis of Oral Tradition.*
Utley, Francis Lee,
1961 "Folk Literature: An Operational Definition", *Journal of American Folklore* LXXIV, 193-206.
Vilkuna, Kustaa,
1968 "Aura, vannas ja ojas" [Plough], *Kalevalaseuran vuosikirja* 48, 108-135.
Wheeler-Voegelin, Erminie,
1949 "Earth-Diver", in Maria Leach (ed.), *Standard Dictionary of Folklore, Mythology, and Legend, I* (New York), 334.